pocket next
page

AN AMUSING GLANCE AT LIFE AND LEADERS IN EARLY COLORADO

by

Michael Yates

Michael Yates.

Mar. 25, 1993

THE GREEN HOUSE PRESS

Fort Collins, Colorado

An Amusing Glance at Life
and Leaders in Early Colorado
by Michael Yates

Design and Typesetting by Jan North-Bishop

First Edition
First Printing

The GREEN HOUSE PRESS
809 Smith Street
Fort Collins, CO 80524

Cover illustration: Owen J. Goldrick (Colorado Historical Society)

Dedicated

to

Betty Yates

ACKNOWLEDGEMENTS

My interest in history and love of politics were responsible for my asking the librarian for a book that concentrated on the early leaders in Colorado. I was told there was nothing among the thousands of books on Colorado politics.

Disappointment turned to enthusiasm when I asked friends and family members about the idea of writing such a book. Everyone I spoke to became excited about the idea.

Once started, the Colorado State University Library, the Fort Collins Library, and the Western Department of the Denver Library were all invaluable.

Jan Bishop, Bea Marvel, Scott Yates, Dennis Gelhouse, and Eleanor Hoague read the manuscript and made constructive and valuable comments.

Finally, I must thank my family and friends who endured my myopic concentration and tolerated my mental absence. For example, Jonathan who rents the apartment beneath me never complained when I caused a small flood by turning on the water for the washer, started typing, and forgot the water. I know what he must have been thinking, but he didnt say anything to the absent-minded guy upstairs.

Dick Yates, David Yates, and Karen Yates have been equally kind. Thanks.

Michael Yates

November, 1992

FOREWORD

If this little book were a boat, it would not stay afloat very long. Railroads and Indians have had only a cursory examination. Cowboys, gunslingers, lawmen, women, and farmers have been almost totally ignored.

Some of the men we visit, like Senator Henry Teller, who would probably have been in the White House if he had represented a more populous state, are outstanding. Time does not diminish their accomplishments. Others, like John Fremont and the Silver King Horace Tabor, may be overrated. Some we look at have not been rated as Westerners at all even though one was responsible for buying the land and another for sending his son-in-law, John C. Fremont, out to explore what the senate had been told was a desert, the kiss of death in the agrarian society in the United States before the Civil War.

Wherever we look, we will see a spirit that permeates Colorados history. Like a bubble, no matter how difficult the circumstances, a true Western hospitality emerged. Perhaps it is best exemplified by the pioneer who recalled an event that probably occurred when Colorado was still Jefferson County, Kansas:

> Once when the baby of an ash hauler died, a friendly carpenter fashioned a coffin from a few clean white boards which the boss gave; the paint shop across the way put on a coat of varnish; somebody found a scrap of clean flannel to line it; a no account boy with a bronco and cart took it to the house all without cost. Those wild west days were not so wild after all. (Hafen, *Colorado And Its People,* Vol. 1, 235)

TABLE OF CONTENTS

Table of Illustrations

TIME LINES

- 1803 Eastern Colorado is acquired by the United States in the Louisiana Purchase.

- 1806 Captain Pike explores Colorado.

- 1820 Major Long explores the front ranges of the Rockies. Congress passes the Missouri Compromise.

- 1825 William Ashley traps in northwestern Colorado. He is responsible for the first Rendezvous of pelt trappers.

- 1842 John Fremont's first expedition to Colorado.

- 1848 Western and southern Colorado is acquired from Mexico.

- 1851 The first permanent settlement in Colorado, St. Louis, is founded.

- 1854 The KansasNebraska Act is passed by Congress.

- 1856 John Fremont becomes the Republicans' first presidential nominee.

- 1858 Green Russell discovers gold in Colorado.

- 1859 John Gregory discovers gold near Central City.

- 1860 Lincoln is elected president.
  First schoolhouse in Colorado erected in Boulder.
  First mint, Clark, Gruber & Company, starts business in Denver City.

- 1861 Congress creates the Colorado Territory.
  William Gilpin is appointed Territorial Governor.
  Civil War begins.

- 1862 First Colorado Cavalry stops a threat by the Confederate Army by decisively winning the Battle of Glorietta in Glorietta Pass, New Mexico.

- 1863 Pioneers in Denver City experience their first fire.

  Telegraph line is completed.

- 1864 Silver is discovered near Georgetown.

  First flood and first grasshopper plague.

- 1870 Kansas Pacific Railroad reaches Denver City.

- 1873 Congress demonetizes currency by removing regulations stipulating the amount of silver required to be minted in coins.

- 1876 Colorado becomes a state.

- 1877 Leadville silver boom begins. Horace (HAW) Tabor acquires the Little Pittsburgh, Crysolite and Matchless mines.

- 1890 Congress passes the Sherman Bill to support dropping silver prices.

- 1891 Winifred Stratton discovers gold at the Independence Mine in Cripple Creek.

- 1893 President Cleveland and eastern bankers repeal the Sherman Act. Populists, a few Democrats and most of the western delegations led by Senator Teller of Colorado attempt to save the Sherman Act by a filibuster against President Cleveland and the Wall Street bankers.

  National panic.

- 1896 William Jennings Bryan gives "Cross of Gold" speech in Democratic nominating convention. He was cheered for two hours. President Cleveland was no even renominated by Republicans. McKinley outspent Bryan ten to one in an exciting presidential race. Senator Teller, a Republican, was so disappointed by the silver issue he supported Bryan in the presidential Race and later became a Democrat. Colorado citizens did not care. They reelected him to the Senate as a Democrat.

AN AMUSING GLANCE AT LIFE AND LEADERS IN EARLY COLORADO

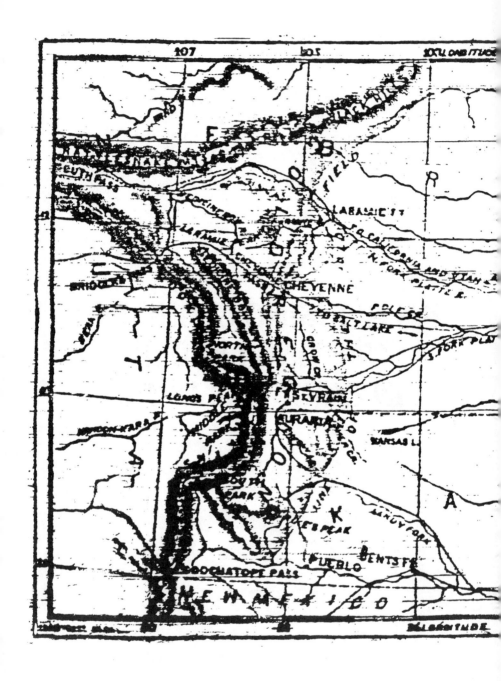

Fig. 1
Map of the Gold Region and Routes Thereto, 1859

In the first issue of the *Rocky Mountain News*, 1859.

Chapter One

MUD AND GOLD

The frontier was hell on women and horses.
—William Byers, Rocky Mountain News

MUD AND GOLD

Zebulon Pike and Stephen Long led the biggest parties to explore the Rocky Mountain region in the early 1800s. Both men explored different areas, and they explored at two entirely different times, Pike sixteen years earlier than Long. Nevertheless, both men concluded that the semi-arid plains area was a desert.

Pike said it would soon be like Africa. Sixteen years later, Long made the same mistake and labeled the Front Range of the Rocky Mountains the "Great American Desert." Long reported to Congress:

> In regard to this extensive section of the country we do not hesitate in giving the opinion that it is almost wholly unfit for cultivation, and of course uninhabitable by a people depending upon agriculture for their subsistence... The whole of this region seems peculiarly adapted as a range for buffalos, wild goats, and other wild game, incalculable multitudes of which find ample pasture and subsistence upon it.[1]

Senator Thomas Hart Benton was dismayed by the desert theory talk. He wanted the country to settle in the West and most important, in California. Benton also believed that Great Britain was poised to swoop down from their outposts in Oregon and occupy California if the United States did not get there first. It was for this reason that he spoke frequently about the people of the United States moving inexorably toward the West. It was our destiny, or, as he said passionately in the Senate, "Manifest Destiny."[2]

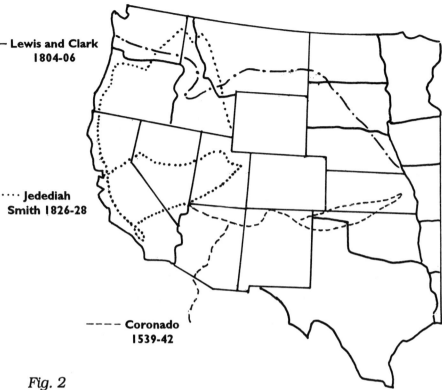

Fig. 2
Some major explorers who avoided the Rocky Mountains.

Pike, sixteen years earlier, was not any help to those favoring Manifest Destiny. His foreboding assessment that the West would in a short time be like Africa did not help the proponents who wanted to hold up the West as a place for the average citizen to pack up his wife, kids, and dog, and move to.

The effect of the misinformation both explorers brought back and reported to the politicians affected the debate for development of the West. In spite of Senator Benton's work toward Manifest Destiny, the desert theory hardened into fact. The desert theory was discussed on the floor of the Senate. This theory had become reality to them since no one since Pike and Long had been to the area to dispute it.

Even though mail to California had to go by ship around the tip of South America, Senator Daniel Webster discouraged a mail route to California through the Rocky Mountains. He cited the facts in the Desert Theory and closed, asking his fellow congressmen:

> What do we want with this vast worthless area? This region of savages and wild beasts of deserts of shifting sands and whirlwinds of dust of cactus and prairie dogs? To what use could we ever hope to put these great deserts, or those endless mountain ranges, impenetrable and covered to their very base with external snow?[3]

Senator Benton could not believe his eyes when he read Long's report about the Great American Desert. First, Pike said the West would soon be like Africa, and now a man sent out to undo the damage to Manifest Destiny returns with a report that the West was only fit for buffaloes and wild goats!

All was not going smoothly at home for Senator Benton, either. His daughter was seeing John C. Fremont. Benton did not encourage their friendship. Everyone in Washington knew that Fremont was literally a bastard. He was pushing thirty, and Jessie was only eighteen. He was only a Lieutenant in the Army, and Benton knew Jessie could do a lot better than Lieutenant if she was patient. Finally, Benton just did not like Fremont. In later years, Fremont would be the first Republican presidential candidate, and Benton would refuse to vote for him and campaign against him. When Jessie asked permission to marry Lt. Fremont, Benton said no.

Fremont took his beautiful Jessie away. They eloped to a Washington Hotel and got married without Benton's permission or blessing. Despite this rocky start it seemed to Benton his son-in-law would be perfect to lead another expedition to the West.

Fremont was in the Army and had learned how to survey land in order to create maps. He had served in the West, and Benton hoped he could be trusted to report on more than the goat population.

Senator Benton crossed his fingers and pushed another western expedition through congress, with Fremont leading it. The large group was made up primarily of mountain men, a few

Fig. 3
Lt. John C. Fremont and William Gilpin. (Drawn by Jan Bishop)

scientists, Fremont's new wife, Jessie, and a stranger Fremont was told to pick up in Illinois. There were thirty-nine in all.

The stranger from Illinois was a tall lawyer, named William Gilpin. Gilpin was devoutly and passionately in love with the West. He sold all his law books for sixty dollars and borrowed a hundred dollars in order to purchase a horse, named "Old Flash," for the trip.

Gilpin's interest in the West was shared by many fellow countrymen. Horace Greeley advised people to go West, and many did. Americans wanted to read heroic adventures about the West, not that it was a desert.

Fremont and his wife Jessie wrote about their Western trips. The first adventure stories were about a hero they called the Pathfinder. Americans were eager for stories about the West. The drama of the Pathfinder stories more than made up for what the expeditions lacked in scientific discovery. Jessie penned the stories because writing made Fremont so nervous "he got nosebleeds from the strain"[4] of writing. He dictated, and she wrote.

Books by or about the Pathfinder were the popular western adventure series of the day. The public loved to read the details about his traveling in this new land west of the Mississippi. In one passage, Gilpin described a Fourth of July celebration with Fremont:

> Three Cheyenne Indians who had attached themselves to the entourage enjoyed the day's festivities... The Indians, impressed with the flag waving, and the booming salute of the Howitzer [gun] Fremont had brashly brought along, enjoyed the barbaric luxury of dining on macaroni soup buffalo meat, fruitcake (made by a relative in St. Louis), and asked Fremont if the American Medicine Days came often. It was a momentous day to be sure.[5]

Benton told Fremont not to take any artillery since he might provoke the Indians. However, Fremont insisted on taking a Howitzer along. The only time it was used was to practice his shooting. Buffaloes were one of his targets.

His most questionable decision was made in the winter of 1848 on his fourth expedition. His guide advised him not to try to cross the central Rockies in December, but Fremont insisted the group make an attempt. The trip was an accident waiting to happen. They did not have enough food or clothing. They got lost in the San Juan Mountains. Eleven men died of exposure and starvation. Fremont and a few others managed to survive by eating the pack animals. Thomas Breckenridge designed a Christmas menu for that year:

BILL OF FARE. CAMP DESOLATION.

MULE

SOUP
Mule Tail

FISH
Baked White Mule

Boiled Grey Mule

MEATS
Mule Steak, Fried Mule, Mule Chops,

Broiled Mule, Stewed Mule, Boiled Mule, Scrambled Mule,

Shirred Mule, French Fried Mule, Minced Mule

DAMNED MULE
Mule on toast (without the toast)

Short Ribs of Mule with Applesauce

(without the applesauce)

RELISHES
Black Mule, Brown Mule, Yellow Mule,

Bay Mule, Roan Mule, Tallow Candles.

BEVERAGES
Snow, Snow-water, Water[6]

After this deadly expedition, Fremont's remarks were self contradictory. He said he had been duped by the guide, and he really did not want to make the trip. Later, he said the trip was a success because it proved that some, if not all, of the expedition had survived.

Fremont's trips to the West stirred the imagination of the country. His public relations value is unquestioned, but few thought his trips had much immediate scientific value. The mountain he discovered was not the highest as he had claimed. Most of the vegetation samples died on the trip home. The biggest disappointment was that the Pathfinder never found a path through the mountains for the mail service or the railroad planners. Even though he had not literally lived up to his Pathfinder nickname, he had helped the hordes of true pathfinders. Many Western pioneers first became interested in the West after reading the exploits of the Pathfinder. Fremont's help was not limited to the inspirational. His surveys helped to make the maps the pioneers used to settle in the West.

The mountain men acted as guides for Fremont and played a big part in his success. The stories about the mountain man, even the term "mountain man," disguised the important part he played in Colorado's history. The mountain man himself was largely responsible for this oversight. After all, he was the one who made up or retold many of the stories. The mountain man was more than the story-book hero who wrestled with bears and outsmarted and outshot the desperado. He was an entrepreneur who realized that with a small financial investment in traps and a lot of courage, it was possible for a man to make a living off a very popular rodent, the beaver.

Beaver pelts first became popular for hats because of the nature of the beaver's fur. Hairs in the fur intertwined with each other. Beaver hats held their shape and were waterproof. As demand increased, pelts rose to $5.00 and sometimes $6.00 each. Most trappers or mountain men averaged between 350 and 400 pelts, for a profit of about $2,000 per year. At first, it was easy to pack hundreds of pelts out of the wilderness, but the good trapping areas moved farther and

Fig. 4
The Mountain Man, Mariano Medina (Fort Collins Public Library)

farther into the forests as the beaver population became depleted. As a result, the mountain man achieved an intimate knowledge of the Rocky Mountains.

A mountain man who married an Indian woman was known as a "squaw man." The Indian family involved encouraged the marriage because the mountain man supported the squaw's family.

Mariano Medina was a mountain man who lived about 40 miles northwest of Denver. A friend of his, named Papin, planned on retiring and returning to the East. He needed horses for the trip, and he also wanted to find a home for his Flathead Indian wife. Papin offered to trade Medina his pregnant wife in exchange for two horses and a blanket:

> Mariano decided this would make a good trade. After all, he could use a woman about his camp to dry the meat, tan the hides, make his garments, pack and unpack the mules, tend his horses, cook his meals, care for his lodge, chop and carry wood and warm his bed.[7]

Trapping tended to be competitive and lonely. It was a never-ending struggle to find out where the beaver were located and to get there before the other mountain men. The one time the mountain men got together to see their friends, exchange tall tales, and share yarns was during the Rendezvous that was held most of the summers between 1825 and 1840. The first Rendezvous was not social. The men returned to the place in which they had buried their furs.

The site of the Rendezvous varied depending on where the beaver were best that summer. Horse racing, story telling, and drinking became almost as important as the pelt trading, but the social aspect was always secondary to the trading. The last rendezvous was in 1840, the same year that pelt prices fell.

One of the true stories that was told and retold at the Rendezvous was about a fellow mountain man, John Colter. He was trapping with an old friend and fellow guide from the

Lewis and Clark expedition. They were in Three Forks country and captured by Blackfeet Indians.

> Potts killed one with his rifle, and was instantly pierced with arrows so numerous he was made a riddle of. Colter was seized, stripped naked, and the manner of his death debated. Instead of using him for a mark to shoot at, the Blackfeet elected to run him. He was given a head start of three or four hundred yards, then the pack pelted after him.... Colter ran mile upon heart-bursting mile to outdistance every brave except one. Unarmed and despairing, he turned upon his pursuer. When the half-exhausted Blackfoot fell in trying to hurl his spear, Colter snatched it up and ran his enemy through, then took to his heels.[8]

Colter ran for two days until he reached the fort. His condition and Potts' body confirmed the truth of his story.

The first organizer to take wagons of supplies into the mountains to trade for the valuable beaver pelts was William Ashley. He was a middleman and wanted to profit from the sale of the pelts but did not want to trap them. He succeeded because he understood the value of trading with the Indians as well as the pioneers. The supplies attracted both the mountain man and the Indian who were saved the long trip out of the mountains to sell their pelts. At the same time both Indian and mountain man could trade for flour, tobacco, and other requirements they needed for the following year.

Trapping had an inevitable consequence: The country started to run out of beavers. This should have increased the price, but the price fell to a dollar a pelt. At the same time the beaver population was almost exhausted, silk hats replaced beaver hats. Nevertheless, the mountain man did not take long to rebound from these unforeseen circumstances. Buffalo robes came into demand, which kept many of the mountain men busy.

Mountain men worked for the cavalry, the explorers, and the wagon trains. Most important, they knew where the passes through the mountains were located. The mountain men discovered the passes for the U.S. Mail Service and the transcontinental railroad. Those routes are still used today by anyone who drives through the mountains near Denver and Cheyenne.

MUD

In 1850 there were a lot of good reasons not to go to Arapahoe County, Kansas. Mountain men did guide wagon trains into the area. The wagon trains used oxen as draft animals because they were cheap and tough, but dumb. If a wagon owner got into his wagon, the oxen would stop and enjoy the pasture. The only way to keep them moving was to walk next to them and snap a seventeen-foot-long bull whip over their heads. This was the job of the bull whacker.

There were no stagecoaches since there were no roads. Railroads had not yet been built. There was only a long, dirty walk of six hundred miles from Leavenworth, Kansas to Arapahoe County, Kansas.

The wagon trains moved so slowly, they seemed to be standing still, but they did average about fifteen miles a day. An advantage of oxen over horses was that Indians never wanted to steal the oxen.

To compensate for the boring walk, the immigrants had a party every night. They mingled, played music on a violin or guitar, and sang songs around the campfire. The mountain man who was guide by day entertained at night. He might recite poetry, or tell about the drought that left the water so low the fish had to stand on their heads to drink. When the people went fishing they took baskets because it was like pulling onions.

The raconteur who told the tall tale was not just telling a joke, or exaggerating the truth. Tall tales were delightful word pictures. A cowboy was not just as strong as all the cowboys in Kansas. That would be dull. A strong cowboy for a mountain man or cowboy might be one who wrestled rattlers bare handed and spotted the snakes three bites at the start. "He knew that he must provide ludicrous imagery, an ingenious piling up of epithets, a sudden transition, a non sequitur, something besides mere exaggeration if his audience was to respond."9

Sometimes another story teller would cap a tall tale. He would tell an even more outrageous story on the same subject. The first man might tell about the time he was camping out, and he felt something cold and heavy on his chest. As he stirred he heard the whir of a rattlesnake, and in the dim moonlight he saw a blunt head with fangs bared, ready to strike.

> He knew that any sudden movement would be fatal. Very quietly he moved his hand toward his six-shooter, always placed within convenient reach. The snake is drawn into an "S," head erect. His hand just closes on the butt of the six-shooter. He draws and fires just as the head is darting toward his face.[10]

That reminded the second man of an experience he had on the Pecos in 1853.

> He woke up in exactly the same fix, except, fool like, he had forgot to put his gun where it would be handy.

> What did he do?

> Well, seeing there wasn't anything he could do, he just shut his eyes and went back to sleep.[11]

The old hands liked to mix word games and jokes in with the yarns and tall tales. The first page of the *Rocky Mountain News* had hundreds of jokes and conundrums, for example:

> What's the psychological difference between killing a man and a hog?

> Assaulting with intent to kill vs. killing with intent to salt.[12]

There was also the recipe for coffee: The cook told the tender-foot to start with two pounds of Arbuckle's Coffee; then add a little water; next, put in a horseshoe; if it sank, add more coffee.

Meals were cooked on the family stove the pioneers were moving to their new home. Since the treeless plains did not provide wood for cooking, the fuel was usually buffalo chips. Pork, canned tomatoes, and coffee as well as beans, potatoes, and hominy were the foods that made up the diet of the immigrants, cowboys, and miners.

Dime novels suggested that the Indian and the Desperado would be dangers they would meet on the trail. However, the most deadly killers were cholera and accidents. One reason for shooting accidents was because of the excessive arma-ments the immigrants brought.

There were also two hundred drownings in an area the pioneers thought was going to be a desert. When they finally reached the Rockies and their destination, there were only a few crude log cabins scattered at random along the Platte River. There were no lawns or gardens. There were no roads, no street lighting, no fire department or police force. Water had to be carried in by the barrel. In most cases the immi-grants left their families at home because of the possible dangers in the move. As a result, there was no one to complain to about deprivations.

What the area did have was dust, dirt floors, and canvas roofs. When it rained, there was no place to go. There was one window in the entire village. The *Rocky Mountain News* stated that in the spring of 1859, there were three hundred log huts covered with mud inhabited by mountain men.

GOLD

For gold to be discovered in this remote region, a butcher, a prospector, and an Indian were as important to each other as the legs on a three-legged stool. John Easter, the promoter, was a butcher who lived in Lawrence, Kansas. He bought cattle from an Indian reservation and knew Fall Leaf, an Indian guide, as a result of his butcher shop business.

Fall Leaf was asked to be a guide for the cavalry on a trip to the Rockies. On this trip he noticed two gold nuggets in a creek. He wrapped them in a rag and stored them until his return to Lawrence. He trusted Easter from previous business dealings in the cattle business, so it was to Easter that Fall Leaf showed the nuggets on his return home. Easter assured Fall Leaf of their value and asked where he got them. Fall Leaf promised Easter he could find the creek again on a second excursion.

The prospectors had no idea where to go. Their only hope was in the assurance of Fall Leaf who had found the gold and said he could find it again. Suddenly, Fall Leaf changed his mind, and said he would not guide a second trip. The miners offered to buy his family a six month supply of food, but he still refused to make the trip. Some think Fall Leaf was afraid and did not feel a small group of prospectors was a safe group to travel with. Others think he did fear for his wife and family. Others favor the theory that he was an alcoholic, and his reasoning was clouded by pioneer rotgut. The answer might be more simple. He might have been afraid he could not find the creek again. No one knows why Fall Leaf did not make the return trip. The prospectors might have wanted to cancel then and there, but they had already bought and paid for six months of provisions. "We all decided to come on and do the best we could under the circumstances."[13]

Two groups from the West and one from the South arrived at what is now Denver in the spring of 1858 to prospect for gold. The men were from all over the country. Green Russell was the leader of the group from Georgia. When they got to what is present-day Denver, there were 104 men.

Most of the men soon gave up and started back toward Leavenworth. On the Fourth of July, 1858, all but Russell, his brother Levi, and eleven others had given up. Russell was the leader of the small group because of his previous prospecting experience in the gold fields of Georgia and California. He kept looking even as others gave up and started home. His tenacity paid off. The small group found placer or surface gold in the sands of Dry Creek, which is Englewood today. There was only a small amount but enough to excite them. They then split up into three groups.

Russell went back for some of the miners who had given up and were traveling east. Levi combined prospecting and shopping for supplies in a trip to Fort Garland. The rest of the men built a log cabin near Cherry Creek. The small settlement about ten miles south of Denver was called Montana City and was convenient to the gold claims near Dry Creek, but the trading routes used by the Indians, explorers, and now miners were next to rivers. The miners decided to build on the land with the Indians where the Platte River and Cherry Creek intersected. They named the town "Auraria," after the Russell brothers' hometown in Georgia.

Winter was approaching. It was about a three-month trip back to eastern Kansas, so a group of miners who wanted to build across the river from Auraria staked their claim to an area they called St. Charles Town Association. In the spring, they would return and build cabins. Just to be on the safe side, they asked two mountain men who lived with their Indian wives in the area to watch their claim and to make sure no one jumped it.

After the founders of the St. Charles Town Association left for their homes in eastern Kansas Territory, a different group of gold seekers led by William Larimer arrived in Auraria in the fall of 1858. Larimer immediately saw the potential in the land claimed by the St. Charles Town Association. He claimed the land for himself. When he was told it had already been claimed, he said that since there were no cabins on the claim, it must have been abandoned. E. P. Stout and Charles Blake supported Larimer in this project to secure the land.

One of the men who was supposed to be protecting the land, William McGaa, said they got his consent after serving him whiskey. He said they took advantage of him while under the influence of the alcohol. The second man, Charles Nichol protested, but he was told he would be hung.

When Larimer, Stout, and Blake claimed the land for themselves, they wanted to change the name, St. Charles Town Association. The questionable way in which the land was acquired prevented a name such as Larimerville or Stout Corners. They sought to dignify the transaction by naming the town after the Governor of Kansas, James W. Denver. Denver had already retired, but there was no way they could have known that at the time. The location at the Platte and Cherry Creek assured Denver's success. Larimer, Stout, and Blake were eventually hailed as great town planners.

Denver and Auraria maintained a rivalry. Each was aware of the other's buildings. They might still be the twin cities of the Rockies, two great cities divided by the Platte, if it were not for the development of Golden.

Golden, 15 miles to the west, challenged the Auraria-Denver City settlement. While the Auraria-Denver rivalry was described as friendly, the rivalry with Golden could be described as cut-throat. This occurred from the outset before the upstart boomtown, Golden, was the Territorial Capitol. The political fights between the towns started over the competition for settlers. Both areas had strengths: Golden was the supply town for miners as it is snuggled against the mountains; Denver and Auraria's location at the confluence of the Platte and Cherry Creek was a decided asset. The cities accounted for the loyalties of the entire Territory. Everyone associated himself with one or the other. Few identified with both. Denver was larger, but Golden was a persistent goad to them to be even better as well as bigger.

Denver City and Auraria instinctively looked toward Golden and were appropriately nervous. They put aside their warm rivalry which up until now had only consisted in counting each others houses and courting immigrants to settle with them. The two agreed to become one city. This agreement was ratified in a moonlit ceremony midway across the Larimer Street Bridge on April 5, 1860. Their new name became Denver City.

In 1858 some traders saw Green Russell panning for gold in Dry Creek. They asked if they could try their luck panning for gold and then got out frying pans. Despite the small amount of ore these men had acquired, when they showed the results to a Kansas City newspaper after returning home, the paper, the *Journal of Commerce* was ecstatic. The headline on August 26, 1858, touted the finding of gold in Kansas Territory.

ARAPAHOE COUNTY

Before the Civil War, the Rocky Mountains in Colorado were the unpopulated western edge of Kansas Territory. If a trapper was west of the Rockies, he was in Utah Territory. If he crossed the Rockies through North Park west of Fort Collins, he would be in Nebraska. Once he reached the Denver area, he would be in Kansas.

There were no farms, towns, or cities. Politicians in eastern Kansas called western Kansas "Arapahoe County" because of the Indians who lived in the area. Congress was not interested in the region until 1858 when gold was discovered in the little-known Arapahoe County.

The settlers in the little city state, which is now Denver, called itself "Jefferson" after Thomas Jefferson, who was a farmer. Even though Jefferson owned slaves, he was personally opposed to slavery. He was responsible for the Louisiana Purchase, the Lewis and Clark expedition, and Manifest Destiny. Jefferson was a "Westerner" before the country had a "West" beyond the Mississippi.

Newcomers to the Rocky Mountains called their new home "Jefferson Territory." Some even pronounced themselves a state and called the region "Jefferson State." The Republicans in Washington, however, were troubled by the name "Jefferson." They observed their mostly Republican western constituents had named their settlement after one of the most important Democrats in history; therefore, a sub-committee declared that only George Washington could have a territory named in his honor.

If not Jefferson, then what name for Arapahoe County, Kansas? The politicians discussed Arapahoe and Yampa, as well as Idaho, Nemara, Colorado, San Juan, Lula, Weapollo, and

Tohasa. Other names considered by the Senators were La-fayette, Columbus, and Franklin. They preferred two of the names: Tohasa and Idaho.

They decided on the name "Idaho" and went home for Christmas. However, the territory had a lobbyist in Washington, and during the Christmas break he pursued the members of the committee and asked them to change the name one more time. On February 4, "Senator Wilson 'at the request of the delegate from that territory' proposed to substitute the name 'Colorado' for 'Idaho.'"[14]

By the time Colorado was formally a Territory, it was late 1859. President Buchanan left the decisions on appointing officials to his successor, Abraham Lincoln.

Lincoln's first appointment for territorial governor was William Gilpin. He had ridden Old Flash on Fremont's first expedition, and he knew the area well. Gilpin's appointment was greeted with joy. The *News* reported parties and dances throughout the Territory. Gilpin gave speeches and was warmly welcomed. Gilpin loved the West, but he was also a military man. After the outbreak of the Civil War, he looked at the map and feared the Rebels could march north. There were no Union troops to block them from taking Denver City and from there the entire West. Rocky Mountain gold could pay for their war effort, and the surge up to Denver City might be the difference in the war.

Gilpin put out a call for volunteers. He had little trouble getting up a regiment since the majority of the Denver citizens were Union supporters. The men were trained near Denver. Cynics called them "Gilpin's Lambs."

The new territory did not have the money for uniforms, food, guns, and all the other expenses that training a small army incurred. As time went by the merchants became more and more vocal about the lambs and their expenses. The federal government, busy with the civil war, ignored Gilpin's pleas for financial support of the First Colorado Cavalry, so he went to Washington to untie the bureaucratic knot. While Gilpin was gone, the merchants signed a petition asking for his removal.

The reason given in the petition was that Gilpin had assumed more authority than he should have by promising that the federal government would repay the merchants for the scrip when the government had not made that promise.

Lincoln bowed to the petitioners, removed Gilpin, and appointed John Evans. Gilpin returned to Denver after pleading the merchants case only to find that he was no longer the territorial governor.

About this same time Major Chivington returned with Gilpin's Lambs from the encounter with the Rebels at Glorietta Pass. Denver City erupted with joy at the news of the victory. The leading citizens Gilpin, Evans, and Chivington shared the same platform when addressing the citizens. Chivington got the most applause. Evans, the new governor, got some applause, and Gilpin got none, but Gilpin showed no hard feelings. It was an ignoble end to his term. The drafts were repaid. His suspicion that the Confederate Army might sweep toward Denver had been correct. He had taken the initiative to train the men, and they had won a clear cut victory. Gilpin had gambled and won, only nobody realized it at the time.

*   *   *   *   *

During this time span, the Concord Coach was the most popular mode of travel. The passengers and drivers rode in comfort. If you rode in a wagon and it hit a rock, *you* hit the rock. If you rode in a Concord Coach and the wheels hit a rock, you did not feel it because of a leather suspension system that acted like shock absorbers.

The baggage was stored in the front and the rear. The coach was reserved for passengers. Rest stops or stations were primitive huts and corrals that were more for the changing and caring for horses than to pamper the passengers. Meals were often cold, and no choice was offered on the menu. If the traveler wanted to brush his teeth, he had to share a toothbrush with the rest of the world. The toothbrush and a dirty towel were securely tied near a dirty pail of water. The Victorian women would sometimes have to sit in the coach with their feet in between the passengers' legs opposite them.

This was called "dove-tailing." The top of the coach was also available for passengers if the inside seats were taken. It was not used for luggage like we see in many of the Western movies.

The Concord was the ultimate in travel. The price for a trip from eastern Kansas to Denver City varied with supply and demand. It was $125.00 for a one way trip before the Gold Rush. The price escalated to $250.00 with increased demand after gold was discovered. Coaches were gaily painted, and the pioneer enthusiasm was reflected in the *News:*

Arrival of the First Express

This is the beginning of the stupendous enterprise...the making of a new road, over a comparatively unknown country... The coaches we have seen are the very best Concord Coaches, finished in the best style, and perfectly new, having never turned a wheel until their departure from Leavenworth.[15]

This stupendous enterprise was front page news. In fact, the News had to run an extra on this issue. Colorado Territory was less isolated politically, and, more important to the lonely young men, it meant MAIL. The 1860 census indicated the discrepancy between men and women in the Territory. It showed there were over two thousand men for each one hundred women, so mail was important. It was also expensive. The government only charged the person mailing the letter three cents, but the person receiving the piece of mail was charged fifty cents for a letter or ten cents for each newspaper. The extra cost went to the delivery company that brought the mail from Cheyenne to the pioneers in Denver City.

The newspapers were recycled by the wives. They saved the old papers and used them as wallpaper in their kitchens. The papers were carefully put right side up and enjoyed for their literary value. They were also appreciated because they kept the wind from blowing through the cracks in the wall. Cowboys lined the walls of their bunkhouses in the same way.

Newspapers were not cheap. Before Denver had a mint to press the miners' gold into coins, the smallest amount anyone could tender was a pinch of gold dust. The pinch was equal to twenty five cents, so the first papers were twenty five cents each. The price dropped to a dime when coins were available.

According to *The Intermountain Press,* the *Rocky Mountain News* raced with another paper to be the first in the Colorado Territory:

> Both papers appeared on the evening of Saturday, April 23, 1859 in the midst of a driving snowstorm. But a self-appointed and excited committee of citizens, rushing back and forth between the two offices, decided that [William] Byers, with the first issue of the *Rocky Mountain News,* had produced a finished paper about twenty minutes before [John L.] Merrick could hand out a completed copy of his *Cherry Creek Pioneer.*[16]

Merrick never printed another paper. He sold his press to Byers at the *News* and tried his luck in the diggings, but returned to Denver broke. He worked for Byers until the Civil War started, then volunteered for the Union army, served with honor through the entire war, and was killed in a brawl in 1865.

Byers later stated: "The Territory of Colorado has five daily newspapers, eight weeklies, and two monthlies, one devoted to Sunday schools and the other to Temperance.... The fact is highly credible to the intelligence and industry of our people."[17]

William Byers was a rawhide-tough combination of crusader and pragmatist. When applying for a job at the *News* it was more important to know how to shoot than how to operate a printing press.

The editor's open warfare against the lawlessness and violence of the pioneer underworld won him many enemies in that quarter. On July 31, 1860, following a printed attack on the notorious Criterion saloon—spoken of as a criterion of every-

Fig. 5
William Byers. (The Denver Public Library, Western History Department)

thing bad—a number of desperadoes who made their head-
quarters there decided it was time to do something about this
troublesome foe. Therefore, primed with liquor and "righteous
indignation" they raided the *News* office and seized Byers.
When his men rallied to his defense with guns, the fearless
editor quieted them and went calmly off with his captors, who
took him to the Criterion. The ruffians were for killing him
without more ado, but the owner of the place, Charlie Harri-
son, was a lodge brother of the editor. He therefore took the
prisoner into a back room and sent him out a rear entrance.[18]

Two ruffians continued the fight. They followed Byers back to
the office, but Byers' partner shot one of them. "Noisy Tom"
Pollack, the town's hangman, shot and killed the second
desperado as he was running away.

Byers would give a person a copy of the newspaper if he did
not have the quarter to pay for it. He retired from the *News* in
1863. The next issue promised the new managers wanted to
be paid in advance.

SOME "FIRSTS" IN COLORADO TERRITORY.

- The first teacher arrived on October 3, 1859:

    The first school in the region was opened at Auraria by
    O. J. Goldrick, a picturesque Irishman, who had ar-
    rived at the settlement some days before. He had
    entered the pioneer town decked out in a silk hat,
    broadcloth suit, and kid gloves, yet driving an ox team
    with the regular bullwhacker's whip. So arrayed he
    naturally had caused considerable amusements but
    soon he adjusted himself to the life of the community. [19]

- The first woman to arrive in Denver was Mrs. Rooker and
  her daughter along with Mr. Rooker from Utah. Mr. Rooker
  finished his cabin on October 27, 1859. [20]

- Two days later, on October 29, 1859, Charles Blake and A.
  J. Williams arrived from Kansas with an ox-train of loaded
  wagons. They opened the first store. [21]

- The first church service in Denver City was poorly attended:

    It was a morning service . . . small. . . . There were no
    church bells to ring, no finely draped ladies, no choir,
    no pews to sit in. But seated on buffalo robes spread
    on the ground, with both the Jones and Smith
    squaws...held the first religious service ever... In the
    opposite end of the cabin I could hear the money jingle
    where the gambling was going on. [22]

- The first telephone in Denver was installed in 1879. It was
  described as the "new system of galvanic muttering machines." [23]

Chapter Two

BLOOD

We have a wolf by the ears, and we can neither safely hold him, nor safely let him go.

—Thomas Jefferson (speaking of slavery.)

BLOOD

"Don't kill him!"[1] someone screamed. Congressman Brooks, however, kept hitting Senator Charles Sumner of Massachusetts until his cane shattered over the senator's bleeding head. After Brooks was pulled off of Sumner, he responded, "I did not intend to kill him, but I did intend to whip him."[2]

Slavery dominated politics before the Civil War. Congressman Preston Brooks of South Carolina attacked Sumner on the floor of the Senate on May 22, 1856, because of an anti-slavery speech Senator Sumner had made. In it he called Andrew F. Butler, Brooks' cousin, the "Don Quixote of slavery," adding that Butler had chosen a mistress to whom he "has made his vows and who, though ugly to others, is always lovely to him; though polluted in the sight of the world, is chaste in his sight. I mean the harlot slavery."[3]

Brooks called this a libel on South Carolina and on Butler, his relative. Congressman Brook resigned in 1856 but was promptly re-elected by his district. Sumner did not die; nevertheless, it was three years before he was able to return to the Senate. The "Bleeding Sumner" episode took its place next to "Bleeding Kansas" as another slavery-related campaign issue.

Slavery had been partially defused in 1820 when Congress passed the Missouri Compromise. Neither side won, but neither lost, because it mandated the 24 states be evenly divided into 12 free states and 12 slave states.[4] The Kansas-Nebraska Act proposed by the Democrats in 1854 made slavery optional in Kansas and divided it into Kansas Territory and Nebraska Territory. The Northern and Western politicians feared that if Kansas and Nebraska became states, they could not be prevented from voting for slavery because they would prefer the cheap farm labor. The balance in the Missouri Compromise would be jeopardized when both Kansas and Nebraska voted for slavery on issues before Congress.

Southern politicians saw slavery as an economic necessity. It was not prohibited in the Constitution, and there was nothing in the Constitution to prevent their leaving the Union. The South believed it was on very strong moral and legal ground. Both sides, the North and West on one side and the South on the other were convinced they were right.

When Stephen Douglas and the other Democrats proposed the Kansas–Nebraska Act in 1854, they did not get rid of the conflict by moving it to the territories. The Democrats divided the country and their own party. The proposed Kansas-Nebraska Act melded together three smaller groups into a party that would soon be defeating the Democrats. The groups, a few Whigs, some Liberty Party men, and a few anti-slavery Democrats, put aside their political differences to meet in a schoolhouse in Ripon, Wisconsin, and agreed to try to stop the bill before it became law. However, if the Kansas-Nebraska Act did pass, they decided they would start another party to try to get the Kansas-Nebraska Act repealed. They named themselves "Republicans." [5]

The Kansas-Nebraska Act became law on May 26, 1854. The Democrats knew that the new law and the Missouri Compromise were incompatible, so on the same day, they passed another bill that stated the Missouri Compromise did not apply in Kansas.

The importance of the bland sounding Kansas-Nebraska Act is far from innocuous. This act awarded the decision on slavery in Kansas Territory to the strongest. The Civil War was fought over states' rights and slavery, but the Kansas-Nebraska Act lit the fuse. Colorado's politics would be almost exclusively Republican for the rest of the 19th century, one more result of the Kansas-Nebraska bill.

Not surprisingly, Kansas Territory split into opposing camps, one slave, one free. They even wrote two Constitutions. The Kansas territory had never known such trouble.

Five months after the passage of the Kansas-Nebraska Act, the Republicans designed their first presidential campaign. The platform demanded the repeal of both the Kansas-Nebraska Act and abolition of slavery in the District of Columbia. The delegates nominated John C. Fremont from Georgia, who had gained his reputation by exploring the West. The Republican slogan for this first effort was "Free Soil, Free Speech, Free Men, Fremont"[6]

John C. Fremont, the son-in-law of Senator Thomas Hart Benton of Missouri, was known as the "Pathfinder" because he had made five different trips to the West, funded by Congress. Americans liked Fremont. The Pathfinder and his stories about his Western trips were very popular. In the South only a tiny minority owned slaves, but the fear of a war between the states swung the election away from the anti-slavery Republican to James Buchanan. The Democrats chose Buchanan because he was available and the "least objectionable" choice.

Republicans in 1856 has some popular issues. They were for homesteading, which was favored throughout the country but had been vetoed by Buchanan. The first Republicans were also for a transcontinental railroad and against annexing Cuba because of its slavery. They reminded the public of the vicious attack on Sumner, but the most important issue was the effort to repeal the hated Kansas-Nebraska Act.

Governor Wise in Virginia warned that if Fremont were elected, there would be a revolution.[7] Afraid of war and the effect that war would have on the economy, New York businessmen did not donate to Fremont's campaign. Horace Greeley, a New York newspaperman with western sympathies, complained the opposition was outspending the "Fremonters" ten to one.

After the nominating convention, Buchanan went home and lived up to the expectations of being the least objectionable

Democratic candidate. He made so few speeches that at the end of the campaign Thaddeus Stevens, a Republican, stated, "There is no such person running as James Buchanan. He is dead of lockjaw."[8]

The Republicans surprised everybody. The new party lost their first bid for the Presidency in 1856 but had made a respectable attempt. They were so close that many observers saw Fremont's loss as a victorious defeat for the new party.[9]

The legislative questions that came out of the slavery question did not stop after Buchanan became President. Slavery absorbed most of the energy of all the people in Washington. The question of Dred Scott, a slave who had escaped to the North and who wanted the same rights as other black citizens in the North, became a volatile issue. Finally, Buchanan and Congress looked toward the Supreme Court to resolve the enigma. After a short deliberation, the court ruled that Scott was to be denied citizenship because his parents were slaves. Then the Supreme Court added that the most useful legislation on the subject, the Missouri Compromise, was unconstitutional.

Reactions to the Dred Scott Decision were predictable. The *New York Tribune* spoke for many Northerners when it said the court had "draggled and polluted its garments in the filth of pro-slavery politics."[10] The South saw the decision as justification for slavery. The *Enquirer* confidently reported: "Abolitionism has been staggered and stunned."[11] The Dred Scott decision and the Kansas-Nebraska Act created a national chasm that neither side could, or wanted, to bridge.

The Democrats in the next presidential election were still split on the slavery question. A Mississippi delegate to their presidential nominating convention put the new relationship succinctly, "We say, go your way, and we will go ours."[12]

In Washington nobody felt safe. Many congressmen, remembering the attack on Sumner, went to the Capitol armed. "By God," cried one, "if I can't talk, I can do something else." [13]

Lincoln got the nomination even though his opponent, Stephen Douglas, had just beaten him two years earlier in a race for the Senate. He was helped by a campaign staff that promised people anything they asked for, including promising one man an appointment to the Cabinet. One of his staff vowed, "We are going to have Indiana for Old Abe, sure."[14]

Stephen Douglas was the first candidate to take his campaign directly to the people, and the people did not like it. The *Northern Iowan* complained, "He [Douglas] demeans himself. .. like one who goes about begging, imploring, and beseeching the people to grant him his wish. . . . He should be attended by some Italian, with his hand organ to grind out an accompaniment."[15]

Lincoln, on the other hand, did not give one speech. He was afraid anything he said would be destroyed by his opponents. The previous successful campaign by Buchanan during which he was accused of lockjaw possibly influenced Lincoln's decision not to speak.

The South warned that if Lincoln were elected, there would be war. The tactic worked against Fremont, but in 1860 Americans outside of the South elected Lincoln by a wide margin. The optimism Lincoln felt on entering office in 1860 dissipated in his term in office because of the Civil War. During most of his term in office, the Union forces did not do well on the battlefield. Few people, including Lincoln, thought he had a chance to win a second term in the 1864 race. Lincoln thought he would get the nomination because "it is not best to swap horses while crossing the river."[16]

In 1863, the Republican party was only eight years old, hardly a Grand Old Party. They simply had not had time to build up party loyalty. In the summer of 1863, the Republicans nominated Lincoln, a Republican, and Andrew Johnson, A Democrat, for Vice President in what looked like an unwinable race. Johnson was against slavery and was one of the few people who supported Lincoln during the Civil War. Some people, like the influential newspaperman Horace Greeley, would have been happy to "change horses," but they did not have enough votes. Lincoln was renominated on the first ballot at the Republican convention.

The radical Republicans were so angry that Lincoln was renominated, they changed their name to "Radical Democracy." They ran their own candidate, John Fremont, the Pathfinder, who had led the Republicans in their first defeat in 1856. The Democrats chose General George McClellan, who had been commander-in-chief of the Union forces until Lincoln fired him because he had the "slows."[17]

During the campaign in 1863 Lincoln's spokesmen accused their

opponents of being defeatists. The radical Republicans turned Radical Democracy and the Democrats spoke of Lincoln's incompetence. It was a dirty, name-calling campaign from the beginning until election day, November 8, 1864. The passionate angry words of the politicians did not deter the leaders of the war.

The election was held without incident. It was the first time in history a country had stopped a wa so that it could vote. General U. S. Grant was prepared for the worst. His telegram to Lincoln may have betrayed his own fears when he stated that "no bloodshed or riot throughout the land, is a victory worth more to the country than a battle won."[18]

Finally, the war was over. Six hundred twenty thousand young men had died. Lincoln looked forward to a life "with malice toward none; with charity for all."[19] Four days later, he was assassinated.

Chapter Three

FIRE, FLOOD, GRASSHOPPERS, AND POLITICIANS

There were times during the 1860s when destructive forces seemed to be in a league against the settlers.1

—Harry Hansen, Colorado: *A Guide to the Highest State*

FIRE, FLOOD, GRASSHOPPERS, AND POLITICIANS

Pioneers were optimists. We know they were young men from looking at census figures. We can see their optimism by watching them react to catastrophes.

Despite the cliche about how some people see a half full glass of water as full and others see it as empty, when the pioneers glass was empty, he saw it as overflowing.

FIRE

After the first major fire in Denver in the middle of a bitterly cold spring night in 1863, Denverites were horrified at losing seventy houses overnight. The flames had destroyed an estimated $197,200 worth of supplies, a serious loss. Denver had volunteer fire departments, but the fire burned the core of the hastily constructed city since a water ditch from the Platte was not completed at that time, which caused a lack of water. The buildings had a political value. Between 1859 and 1863, Auraria and Denver City competed with each other and the other boom towns. Key words in advertisements to sell lots were minister, church, and school. Houses, or the lack of them, determined where new immigrants would settle.

The *News* later reported:

> The city bounced back [from the fire] with enthusiasm as it contemplated the new construction that would replace the old, congratulating itself that the new buildings would be largely of brick and stone, instead of wood that fragile and combustible material that identified the buildings of a pioneer town.[2]

It did not take long for these good intentions to mature into actions that resulted in a stunning city. The only trees were a few cottonwoods and willows on the banks of the Platte, so it was inevitable that brick and stone would replace wood as the primary building material.

A young man riding a Concord coach looked out the window and wrote home in June, 1866:

> Suddenly I perceived through the dust a stately square Gothic tower and rubbed my eyes with a sense of incredulity. It was really true; there was the tower built of brick well proportioned and picturesque. Dwellings and cottages rose over the dip of the ridge, on either side brick blocks began to appear, and presently we were rolling through gay, animated streets . . . [3]

This letter was written three years after the fire. The fire was only the first of several disasters that Denver City had to overcome in its first years.

FLOOD

Indians warned the pioneers not to settle near the Platte and Cherry Creek. It seemed the Platte was a mile wide and an inch deep, but the Indians told the pioneers that the river could and did flood. The pioneers ignored the advice and moved into the most vulnerable area. The first time the pioneers were flooded occurred almost one year to the day after the fire. It was estimated the flood caused up to $1,000,000 in property damage.

The *News* could not report about it because it had been wiped out by the flood. Byers and his family lived in the same building in which his press was located. Discouraged after losing all his personal possessions, he asked his wife if she wanted to return to Iowa. She said no because the area needed a paper. [4]

The first school teacher, Professor Goldrich, who had arrived in town driving a team of oxen he cursed in Latin, was asked to write an account of the flood for *The Denver Commonwealth.* The *Commonwealth* helped the *Rocky Mountain News* until it acquired another building. Later, the *News* helped the *Denver Post* when it was flooded.

Fig. 6

Cherry Creek Flood, May 19, 1864. (Denver Public Library, Western History Department

On the night of May 20, 1864, the waters of Cherry Creek rose, and a wave of water swept down the valley, carrying with it the *Rocky Mountain News* office Byers had diplomatically placed between the once rival towns of Denver City and Auraria. The City Hall and all the records stored there as well as eleven lives were lost in the flood.

The pioneers did not miss their former City Hall. Like most civic buildings in boom towns, it was hastily put together with wood, and the records of births, deaths, weddings, and property ownership were vulnerable to fire and, in this case, flood. The pioneers looked forward to building a better City Hall.

GRASSHOPPERS

About six months later the settlement was surprised again with another natural catastrophe. Three years earlier they had to import almost all their food from Kansas. Wagon trains brought in tons of supplies, but the prices were higher because of the trip. There were few fresh fruits and vegetables available on the front range.

Byers was from Iowa and was convinced the future of Colorado did not lie in its mining riches but in its agriculture. He sold vegetable seeds at 25 cents per packet and proudly announced the first fresh Rocky Mountain grown radish on August 24, 1860.

Three years later the small truck farms had grown a crop big enough to meet the demand of the immigrants and miners. Just before this crop could be picked the grasshoppers came. Like the floods and fires, they would be a recurring nightmare for the pioneers. The worst plagues were in 1864 and later in 1870 and 1874. Thousands of the grasshoppers hatched on local farms while millions came in migrating clouds. The *Central City Register* described one incursion:

> As the sun reached the meridian today, countless millions of grasshoppers were seen in the air while the atmosphere for miles high was literally crammed with them. They sailed by under the pressure of a light east wind in vast billowy clouds, the lower strata falling in a ceaseless shower on the ground, covering the streets,

sidewalks, the exterior of buildings, jumping, crawling, crushed by every passing foot, filling the eyes and ears, and covering the garments of pedestrians, swarming everywhere in irrepressible currents.[5]

Colorado was not the only victim of grasshoppers. Kansas, Nebraska, and other states to the east suffered as much or more, and the federal government even made a "grasshopper appropriation" or feeding and clothing destitute farmers.

POLITICIANS

The first pioneers were angry at both Kansas and Washington for ignoring the front range. They called themselves the Jefferson Territory or Jefferson State, but they were not a Territory or a State and not treated as either by Washington.

The pioneers wanted some basic services and were disappointed when Washington, distracted by the Civil War, ignored Jefferson Territory. One letter home summed up the frustration:

> This Rocky Mountain Country . . . has received about as much legislative aid at Washington as the Fe Gee Islanders. No mail service for the next 12 months that can be relied on; no extinguishment of the Indian Title; no territorial organization; and in fact, no sort of governmental recognition for the advancement of our interests here . . . so we are compelled to adopt the squatter sovereignty doctrine, making our own laws.[6]

William Byers described a politician in one of the humor columns of the first *Rocky Mountain News* in 1859. "A politician is one who buoyant by putrefaction, rises as he rots."[7]

Colorado Territory was not created until 1861. In the interval the pioneers made up laws as they went along. The Miners' Districts protected the prospectors. Claim Clubs were used by the farmers. Peoples Courts enforced the rest of Frontier Justice.

These formal forums provided the basis for the "Jefferson Territory" Constitution. That Constitution was the basis for Colorado Territory's Constitution, and that document was the model for Colorado's present Constitution. Some current laws, such as those about water, go straight back to a nineteenth century miner who simply wanted to protect his claim from the other prospectors.

A reporter noted the need to formally write the peoples intentions. He observed:

> Making governments and building towns are the natural employment of the migrating Yankee. He takes to them as instinctively as a young duck to water. Congregate a hundred Americans anywhere beyond the settlements, and they immediately lay out a city, frame a State constitution and apply for admission into the Union, while twenty-five of them become candidates for the United States Senate.[8]

In Denver, the first volunteer legislators were elected in 1858. They held a thirty day session that convened in November 1859. This "Jefferson" legislature enacted provisions for officer's salaries, a judicial system, and the creation of counties. It was this group that passed the one dollar poll ta the miners had rebelled against.

The miners refusal to pay the tax was a significant problem for "Jefferson Territory." When the federal government created "Colorado Territory," the legislators had the authority to impose a one dollar poll tax but only asked fifty cents.

Aside from a lack of money, the young territory had some bitterly contested legal questions. One was who would get roads. The present setup involved mountain men who charged whatever they felt like for a settler to cross his river or use his road. The second problem to work out was to determine which cities got the railroad. No tracks had been laid in Colorado Territory, but it was obviously going to be the modern and more desirable mode of travel. Every politician argued that the tracks should go through his district. Finally, the young government needed to decide where the Territorial Capitol should be located. Golden, Colorado City, and Denver City each thought it was a suitable city for this honor. Later, when the Silver boom starts, Leadville's mayor, Horace Tabor, wanted the Capitol to be in Leadville.

The new government could not afford to build roads for the stages and lay tracks for the railroad. After a great deal of debate the result was a type of geographical compromise. The log-rolling ended up with Denver and Colorado City's getting the most. They split the railroad and the capitol. Denver would start laying tracks toward Kansas, and Colorado City got the state capitol. At first, Golden and the miners got nothing. The Golden residents resented the Eastern politicians taking both the railroad line and the state capitol.

* * * * *

Two of the most prominent citizens shared the same cabin. "Uncle Dick" Wooten moved into Auraria from New Mexico a few months before Byers. His arrival was a memorable one for many of the pioneers who lived in Auraria and for the miners who were crowded into the settlement until warm spring weather would allow them to return to their claims in the mountains.

Wooten arrived on Christmas morning, set up his tents, and began a thriving business. He knocked in the head of a barrel of pioneer rotgut called Taos Lightning. He put out some tin cups and invited the community to "dip in." Little more needed to be said:

> All Auraria soon called, and the news spread across to Denver City...The flowing contents of that barrel acted as a dove of peace. It submerged the last vestige of rancorous rivalry between the two cities; and also a number of worthy citizens.[9]

Aside from being a cagey retail salesman, Wooten had been a trapper, a farmer, and a shepherd. He singlehandedly drove a thousand sheep from New Mexico across the Rockies, over the desert, and into California, losing only one hundred sheep.

When he moved out of the tent and into a cabin, it was particularly luxurious. There were two stories. It had a wooden floor and the only window in town, which is why Byers rented the second floor for his fledgling *Rocky Mountain News*. Wooten and Byers shared the same philosophy about government. Both thought a vigilante committee was the answer for

"Old Fashioned Justice." Politics were simple. There was no recognized government at the time, but the rules were clear.

Stealing of any kind was not a safe business, and committing a crime against property brought certain punishment. There were three grades of punishment for different types of criminals. For minor offenses the punishment was thirty-nine lashes on the bare back of the offender. For the most serious offenses the punishment was death. There was a third option if the culprit was a known bad man and the court could not decide on whipping or killing: "We notified him to leave the country and he always found that the only safe thing to do was to go."[10]

Few of these penalties called for jail time because there were not many jails. A desperado might be tied to a tree, handcuffed to a telephone poll, or put in a dry cistern. In one instance in Gilpin County, the Sheriff took two horse thieves home and shackled them to a bed. The next morning, his wife who was in bed with a sick child, made such a fuss that the Sheriff went out that day and got some street loafers from Central City to build a small stone jail.

Criminals were hung from whatever was handy — a tree, or in the treeless plains of Colorado, railroad trestles. The vigilante or vigilance committees did not spend all their time looking for someone to string up. Most of the time it was enough to threaten the use of the committee to accomplish what was needed. The *News* warned:

> CAUTION. —On Wednesday night last two individuals who are well known, busied themselves by furnishing whiskey to some of the Indians camped in town. We give them notice that there is a Vigilance Committee of long standing still in existence here, which is pledged to lynch any man found engaged in giving or selling intoxicating liquor to the Indians and thus endangering the safety of the settlers. Once more gents, and you will see the operation of the people's prohibitory law.[11]

This "caution" was used frequently by Byers. He usually assured the culprits that he knew who they were, which probably had the desired effect because there were no more warnings in the next paper.

Citizens of Denver were protected by a number of organizations, each with its own uniform. The most popular was the "Jefferson Rangers" It was a volunteer group made up of professional men within the community. They drilled in their handsome uniforms and performed the functions of a city police force.

James Gordon asked a man to have a drink with him at a bar. The man refused. Gordon shot him dead. Gordon may have had the best-attended hanging in Colorado history since it was witnessed by several thousand people who were kept in order by the Jefferson Rangers. There were probably a few political stump speeches before Gordon was hung.

In the East, political machines helped the candidates get elected. These well-oiled patronage machines worked best in cities where class lines are relatively distinct. [12] However, in the Territories the pioneers were classless and proud of it. Social classes were impossible to find. Everyone wore work clothes and beards, and to make it even more difficult, most had adopted a second name. Social classes were difficult to recognize even after miners struck it rich. Pictures of boom towns near working mines show all the men visiting and shopping in identical three piece black suits and bowlers, resembling a convention of bankers.

With no political machine to help, the western candidate for Sheriff or legislator had to campaign by himself. These stump speeches took him to wherever he could find a crowd. He went into mining camps, saloons, horse and trotting races, barbecues, and churches. He knew the frontiersmen had a natural lack of trust for politicians:

> The cowboy gets up early in the morning, decides what to do, then straddles his pony and gets to work. He does the best he can and spends as little money as possible.
>
> The politician gets up late in the morning, straddles the fence, spends all the money he can get, gets all the votes lined up, and then decides what to do. [13]

or:

Said a store keeper to his competitor, "I guess we'll have to close up Monday next. Why?"

"Senator Blank is going to be in town."

"My God, has he taken to stealing in the daytime? "[14]

or:

A man hired a lawyer to represent him in a damage suit. After months of litigation, he secured a judgment for $2,000. The lawyer handed him a silver dollar.

"What is that for? asked the client."

"That is the balance coming to you after deducting court costs and attorneys fees."

"What's the matter with this dollar? Is it counterfeit?"[15]

or:

R. M. Williamson, a judge known as Three-legged Willie, told of the time he was commissioned by the president of the Republic of Texas to hold court in a county where a feud had been raging for some time, and where no court had been held, for each faction had reason to fear indictments.

Just before the time set for court, the inhabitants laid aside their differences long enough to hold a mass meeting and adopt a resolution that court should not be held. When Williamson took his seat at the bench, a man arose, read the resolution, and moved that court adjourn. The judge asked him if he could cite any law for such a proceeding. The man stepped forward, drew a large Bowie knife, and laid it on the table, saying, "This, your Honor, is the Statute."

Now the Colt revolver had just been perfected and placed on the market. Three-legged Willie drew a .45 six-shooter and said, "And this is the Constitution which overrides the Statute. Open court, Mr. Sheriff, and call the list of grand jurors for the term."[16]

or:

Attorneys who had gone to law school, especially the ones who had taken the optional bar exam chafed when the judge was a doctor, miner, or a saloon keeper with no background in the law.

An attorney closed a long and involved argument with the statement that such and such a court decision, with which the court was no doubt familiar, should govern the case.

The judge, who knew very well how he was going to rule, court decision or no court decision, replied that he made it a point to know as little law as possible. "Your Honor has succeeded admirably," retorted the attorney.[17]

Chapter Four

The Sack

By God, now my wife can be a lady.[1]
—John Gregory, after first pan of gold,
May 6, 1859

THE SACK

Much of the West's growth was of storybook propor-tions. Green Russell took his finger out of the dike, and thousands flooded into Colorado Territory. Americans, suffering through the violence resulting from the Kansas–Nebraska Act, a recession, and a decade-long drought in Kansas during the 1860s, read about the new el dorado at the foot of Pikes Peak. The myth that was selling newspapers was that gold was just lying around in the Rocky Mountain area. One pilgrim took an empty sack and told his wife he would just fill up the sack and come home. Manufacturers soon found the most effective way to sell their spoons, glasses, shovels, gold pans, and any other merchandise was to stamp "Pikes Peak or Bust" on it.[2]

Mining pamphlets and maps were written by people who had never been west of the Hudson. It was a glorious story that made everybody happy. The businessmen loved it. Adventurers loved it. Those wanting to escape the violence generated by the Kansas–Nebraska Act loved it. Song writers and poets loved the idea of gold just everywhere.

Hordes of people went in wagon trains to the new territory. Some walked with backpacks. Others pushed handcarts and wheelbarrows. Some hung sails off wagons. Most of these "wind wagons" did not get far, but one got to Denver, and another was within 40 miles of Denver when a strong wind caused the wagon to crash. There is no proof of this episode because, according to legend, no one was hurt, and they left the wagon on the side of the road and walked in.[3] One man had six dogs pulling a cart; another was seen being towed by two young men. Each had his own empty sack to fill up. Another optimist filled his cart with empty flour sacks.

There were so many hopefuls, so any dreamers.

At night prairie campfires were visible in an east-west panorama that sometimes stretched from horizon to horizon.[4]

Half of the estimated 100,000 men reached the Rockies. The other half left their empty gold sacks on the desolate plains and went home. Nobody told them about the trip to the gold, and if anybody had told them, they were not listening. The *Missouri Republican* saw the traffic going through their state, not to it, and observed:

> . . . steamboat[s], hundreds after hundreds of them from every place—Hoosiers, Suckers, Corn crackers, Buckeyes, Red-Horses, Arabs, and Egyptians . . . Enthusiastic, merry, with light hearts and a thin pair of breeches, they calculate to accomplish all their fondest hopes.[5]

When some of the disappointed immigrants started coming home, the cities that were worried about their own populations emigrating to the gold fields in the west cheered. The *Hannibal Messenger* reported: "An extra train of 'Pikers' came in about 2 o'clock yesterday afternoon. Whew! But warn't they mad!"[6] The editor implied he knew all along that the mad rush to the Rockies was:

> . . . the humbug of humbugs . . . The Spectacle of 100,000 people simultaneously abandoning all the comforts, conveniences, and endear-

ments of home, and setting out, many of them on foot, and without a dollar in their pockets, and with barely provisions to last them a week, upon a journey from five hundred to a thousand miles, over a wild and inhospitable region, all animated and almost run-mad with gold greed; and then, after a lapse of a few weeks, coming back, begging, starving, cursing, and many of them hopelessly ruined, is one never before witnessed, and one that teaches such a lesson as in our opinion, will prevent repetition of a similar act of folly for a long time to come.[7]

The editor of the *Hannibal Messenger* might not have had such a brutal welcome home if he had known about the horses and cattle that had starved to death. He probably did not know that more men and women went insane because of the hardships of the trip than were murdered by Indians.

He did not see these pioneers sit quietly on the side of the trail and die of exhaustion. Their bones littered the side of the trail. The fact is that a full half of the pioneers actually made the grueling three month trek and reached the front range of the Rockies. Unfortunately, they looked for gold in Englewood and on Pikes Peak. The placer gold was quickly picked up, and the gold inside Pikes Peak would remain there until a persistent cowboy named Bob Womack discovered its secret.

Many of the newcomers started the return trip to their homes in Kansas. If they had been tricked, they jumped to the conclusion that it was William Byers who deceived them in the *News*. Byers was a natural to be the scapegoat. His paper published rumors of gold strikes and printed a "Map of the GOLD REGION with Routes Thereto" in the first issues of the *News*. He could have misled the whole world into moving to the Rockies, but he did not think one needed to lie about the area in order to persuade people to move there. He was honest to a fault. The man who wrote scathing editorials about murderous thieving Indians and idiot Democrats was not going to stretch the truth about his beloved Colorado. Byers covered the topic on September 21, 1863, in an editorial:

Big Stories

If you want to see a story grow, just whisper to some one in confidence that Hr. [Honorable] A. _____ arrived from Bannack last night with a handsome little sum in gold dust, and then watch the corners. If the story don't come back to you inside of three hours so magnified that you wont know it, then we don't want a cent.[8]

If the pioneers could not find gold but wanted to stay in the area, they were in luck. Denver had a need for workers, or they could also go into business for themselves. A tavern was often a sign on the back of a wagon or a sign on the front of a tent and a limited amount of beer or whiskey. After Horace Tabor had made his fortune, he said pioneer beer was only good for washing goats.

Gamblers had a symbiotic relationship with the saloons. Brothels prospered in a community made up almost totally of men. Newspapers opened and closed as fast as the towns opened and closed. They exposed slippery politicians, horse thieves, and claim jumpers. The *News* kept a list of the newcomers and where they were from. The paper also helped the newcomers get started by telling them where to go for their own needs, such as room, board, and supplies, and where to trade their tired oxen for horses or mules.

The papers were also a source of humor, opinion, international news, and stories. They boosted their own community and bragged about improvements:

> Dr. Avery whose Dental Room is in Fish's new block, upstairs, has just received a Dentists Chair of the modern style. This was all the doctor lacked to complete his outfit. Resting in that luxurious piece of upholstering, one could submit to sawing, filing and plugging of his bicuspids or having a tooth yanked, without shrieking like a Sitting Bull or roaring like a Sea Lion.[9]

The ministers were not far behind the first influx of settlers. Many were Methodists. They rode the circuit. One Methodist, the Reverend John L. Byer, walked to Denver from Minnesota.

He reached Denver on June 20, 1861. He then walked to Fairplay in order to save the $2.45 coach fare. By the end of 1861 he had walked five hundred miles and collected $45.00 in contributions. He was called Father Dyer because of his grey hair.

Most circuit riders preferred to ride. This allowed the visiting minister a chance to repeat his favorite hell fire sermon over and over to different congregations. Riding had an unexpected benefit for a circuit rider in Pueblo. The minister just left. It is hard to tell if the letter writer is happy or sad, but he certainly is surprised:

> Pueblo's one minister has left. He couldn't stand the racket. He was willing to try most anything, the Fee Gee Islands, interior Africa, the hottest corner of perdition, if need be, but he couldn't go Pueblo. Hence, the Heathen rage as before, and we don't know why.[10]

Another minister, a Baptist from New York, sought out sinners in saloons as well as churches. After his visit to Central City, one resident wrote to the editor of the paper that "this worthy brother's labors are hardly free from blame and worldliness . . . Christianity depends for its success upon its divine founder and needs no claptrap or eccentricity to advertise it."[11]

Central City is not the center of Colorado. Central City was originally Centre City because it was between the Gregory Diggings and the lodes in Nevada Gulch. Mining towns were central to the growth of Colorado. Central City is Colorado's oldest surviving mountain city. [12] The mining towns were also indispensable to the miners.

Luck and endurance had more to do with mining success than skill or training. Governor Routt went as broke as the next man. He had to borrow to keep working a claim of his in Leadville. He kept shoveling and eventually he, too, made the claim pay off while he was in office. When silver got him out of debt, he hired two men to work his claim while he stayed in Denver and received a good return for his efforts.

Success often went to tenderfeet who had no idea of how to prospect for gold. Two pharmacists from Colorado Springs got to the diggings and did not know what to do or where to go. They simply threw a hat in the air and claimed the land around where it had landed. The old timers scoffed until they saw the newcomers had dug into one of the richest veins in the mountain. They called it the Pharmacist Mine.

Horace Greeley described the area for the *New York Tribune:*

> As yet the entire population of the valley —
> which cannot number less than four thousand,

including the five white women and seven squaws living with white men — sleep in tents, or under booths of pine boughs, cooking and eating in the open air. I doubt that there is yet a table or chair in the diggings.[13]

The little creek trickling down the south side of the majestic Pikes Peak in Poverty Gulch was dangerous for the cattle. A letter arrived from England addressed to "Lame Creek." There was no trouble finding the addressee in Cripple Creek.

On their first mad rush to Pikes Peak, the pioneers did not find gold. Bob Womack was a cowboy who prospected in the area. He even built a shack so he could spend all his free time looking for gold. Womack was an easy going cowboy. His boss complained he wasted too much time looking for gold. He was alone in the mountains, so he tried to make up for lost time when he came to town. "He could punish any amount of bad whiskey, and whenever he came to town, other people had to stand aside."[14]

Bob Womack was the first to discover gold in Pikes Peak. Much like Green Russell, Womack kept looking for gold when the consensus was very clear that no gold was there. When he finally discovered gold and had it analyzed, the first reaction of most of the people in Colorado Springs was one of suspicion. However, it was real gold, and the timing for Colorado could not have been better. His discovery was the economic salvation for the state in 1891. His pasture was transformed into a boom town.

Bob Womack's success in Pike's Peak was topped by the more serious Winfield Stratton. Stratton took young Billy Fernay into the mountains with him. The two purchased two mules at Manitou. One of the mules became obstreperous and cut himself on some barbed wire. The animal refused to move, so Stratton beat it with a long board. Women who had observed his method of behavior modification for the mule called the humane society.

"Interfering, gossipy women,"[15] muttered Stratton as the two ran to avoid the clutches of the Humane Society. While they were avoiding pursuit, the other mule, the one carrying all the dynamite, ran for a tree and started to scratch himself. Stratton and Fernay ran in the opposite direction, fully expecting the mule to blow himself up, but he did not.

One of Stratton's idiosyncrasies was his firm belief that only as much ore as one needed should be taken from the mountain. He had good luck with his Independence Mine. The British company that bought it, however, had no such scruples. They made Stratton the first millionaire miner. They paid him $10,000,000 for the Independence Mine.[16]

In 1894 the Cripple Creek business directory had almost 800 businesses. The businessmen were proud when a nationally famous journalist, Julian Street, offered to visit and report on the boom town. Later, Street complained he was not feeling well because of the altitude. He admitted in the article that this weakness prevented him from seeing the sights of Cripple Creek. He did not feel well enough to leave the immediate neighborhood, which was where the parlor houses were located. The houses on the streets had names, e.g., Clara, Louise, Tina, etc., rather than numbers. He made Meyer Street nationally famous. He wrote that Cripple Creek was extremely depressing because of smokestacks, squalid shanties, ore dumps and the like.

The miners were horrified at his description of Meyer Street, but Cripple Creek had the last word. They changed the name of Meyer Street to Julian Street.

TABOR

Leadville is west of Cripple Creek. The only thing separating them is Mosquito Pass. Leadville became nationally famous because of the silver boom and the Silver King, Horace Austin Warner Tabor, or Haw (an acronym from Tabors first three names). His was one of the most compelling rags to riches stories in Colorado.

The Horace Tabor stories usually start when he was about fifty, and most accounts ignore his first wife, Augusta. The stories begin when he owned a store in Oro City. Some add, incorrectly, that he was poor before striking it rich. It is said that he sponsored two prospectors who, while negotiating the terms of a loan, stole a bottle of whiskey from his store. The prospectors did not go far or dig much because of the effects of the whiskey. Some accounts have them discovering silver two feet down in a wonderful example of serendipity.

Augusta Tabor kept a diary and wrote letters. She was even a member of the Colorado State Press Association. Thanks to Augusta, the early part of her and Tabor's marriage is well documented. Both of them were originally from New England. Tabor worked for Augusta's father as a stone cutter in Maine. They moved to Kansas Territory so they could qualify for the Homesteading Act. According to the new Republican law, Tabor would be entitled to 160 free acres of land if he built a farm and worked it for three years.

Augusta had come from a comfortable home that had both a cook and a maid. She was the eleventh woman to settle in Colorado Springs and one of the first to move to Kansas. She was uncomfortable after the move to Kansas, confessing in her diary:

> I shall never forget the morning of my arrival. To add to the desolation of the place, one of the Kansas winds was blowing furiously. Sitting upon an open prairie, one half mile from any cabin, was my future home— a log cabin, 12 by 16 feet; not an outhouse, or a stone, or stick in sight. I was ushered in and the only piece of furniture in the place was a Number 7 cook stove that was confiscated from the Border Ruffians' brotherhood. I sat down upon an old trunk, the only thing to sit on, and the tears began to flow copiously.[17]

Tabor was grateful to the Free Staters for the cabin, and for the first time in his life, he adopted a political preference. He enthusiastically helped the Free Staters who had built the cabin for Augusta and him. The Free Staters hoped that if families moved to Kansas, they might stay there. They helped the young Tabors.

Kansas had split into two governments because of the Kansas-Nebraska Act. The Free Staters were against slavery, which suited Tabor. He ran for the legislature of the anti-slavery party and was elected a representative in the Free Kansas Territory. About this same time another Free Stater, John Brown, murdered five men. President Pierce tried to quiet the trouble in Kansas that had resulted in two warring factions by outlawing one of the two parties. The President outlawed the Free State party because of John Brown's violence. As a result of representing a political party the government had prohibited, Tabor was labeled a traitor.

Tabor joined some other Free Staters who had been elected to the anti-slavery party in Kansas. In the summer of 1856, he went to Topeka to be sworn in as a legislator in spite of the order from President Pierce. On the morning of a sunny Fourth of July, Tabor solemnly entered the clapboard shack with the others in order to be sworn in.

The Union was ready to stop the Free Staters. If they would not stay home and insisted on this meeting, Col. Edwin Sumner would stop them. After they entered the shack, Col. Sumner ordered his five companies of soldiers to surround the hall. There were two pieces of artillery that were also available. In response, the Free Staters prepared for hostilities.

Promptly at noon the clerk called the roll. Only seventeen answered when their names were called. There was not enough for a quorum. Col. Sumner read a proclamation from President Pierce asking the crowd to disperse. The people gave Col. Sumner a cheer and then left.

Augusta was unhappy with farm life in Kansas because she was afraid of snakes, and there were uncounted numbers of snakes in the Kansas Territory. She wrote that it was not unusual for Mr. T. to kill twenty a day. Horace and Augusta did not like Kansas, the farm, the political climate, or the drought in Kansas Territory, but they did produce their only child, Maxcey, a son, at that time. When Tabor heard rumors in Fort Riley about gold being found in the Rocky Mountain area, both he and Augusta made plans to move. She hoped no other place could have as many snakes as Kansas.

Tabor brought two buddies with him to Kansas. They had eagerly agreed to accompany him on the trip to the West. Tabor had worked as a stone cutter in Fort Riley to make the necessary money for the long trip. After two months of saving, he, his friends, Augusta, and a

Fig. 7
Augusta Tabor (The Denver Public Library, Western History Department)

sick teething baby struck out for the West with several milk cows. Once in Colorado, Tabor and his friends wasted no time looking for California Gulch. Augusta wrote in her diary:

> Leaving me and my sick child in the 7 x 9 tent that my hands had made, . . . left on the morning of the glorious Fourth (of July). My babe was suffering from fever and I was weak and worn. My weight was only ninety pounds. How sadly I felt . . . twelve miles from a human soul save my baby.[18]

Three weeks later Tabor returned to the tent empty handed. He had not even found the trail to the established gold diggings, much less any gold. He then decided to go to Russell Gulch. After three more weeks that did not produce any profits, the Tabors moved to Payne's Bar, or present day Idaho Springs. Augusta was the first white woman, "if white I could be called, after camping out for three months."[19]

This time the men built her a four foot wall on which she could place her tent, and left her again. Anticipating the men would return with big appetites and little else, Augusta opened the first of a series of small but profitable ventures. She sold pies and milk.

When Tabor and his friends returned, Augusta had a thriving business established with the prospectors. She made enough to pay off the debts on their Kansas farm. Tabor did not want to return to farming. He disagreed with Augusta over the way she spent her profits.

Tabor finally dug into what looked like a good claim. He was advised by a friend to move to Denver because snow slides might be a danger to his family. He moved out of the mountains and spent the winter in Denver with Augusta and Maxcey.

They lived on the pie profits that had not gone to Kansas to pay off debts. In the spring,he returned to the mountains only to find his friend was actively mining his claim. It was a serious breach of the Mining District laws. It was a crime punishable by hanging, but Tabor let him have the valuable claim and returned to Denver to plan another trip.

This time the Tabors moved south. They both liked Colorado Springs. Horace and Augusta had to move from that site because no one else lived in the area.

Tabor eventually gave up prospecting for gold, and joined Augusta in retail sales to the prospectors. The Tabors were respected and their store, gold dust transport business, boarding house and post offices all were vital to the miners in Buckskin Joe and Oro City.

When the towns moved to follow the latest gold rumors, the Tabors had to move, too. The miners helped move the entire store. It was because of the store that Tabor was chosen to be Lake County Treasurer.

Oro City was growing and Tabor was unhappy with the name "Oro," which meant "ore." The town was one of the most picturesque and wealthy in the country. In a vote that included Mountain City and Leadville as well as Oro City, the majority supported changing the name to Leadville.

When it was time for the new town to elect its first mayor, Tabor had little competition. He won the first special election, and the first regular election two months later.

The small ventures that Augusta had started to compensate for Horace's lack of skill or luck as a prospector made the Tabors one of the most prosperous families in the area. Their store was so busy they needed to hire two people just to help in the post office.

Another reason Tabor was popular was his inability to say no. Whenever anybody wanted a loan or grubstake they would go to Tabor. Augusta did not like to see him giving away the profits, but it did not surprise her. Horace never said no to the Free Staters in Kansas. He could not say no to the so-called friend who jumped his claim, and now with the contents of a store to give away he was not about to learn.

On Sunday, April 21, 1878, while he was sorting mail, two German prospectors, August Rische and Theodor Hook, walked into the store. They told Tabor about their plans and needs. First they borrowed $17.00 worth of food supplies. A few days later, they returned to borrow another $60.00 for tools. Tabor had them sign in a book and promise to pay him back one third.

Rische and Hook had not been lucky before arriving in Leadville. They had gone through their savings looking for gold and had to work in mines for wages. After patiently digging 27 feet, they found what they were looking for. The next thing to do was report the good news to their partner at the Tabor store. Augusta was on duty and sorting mail. She wrote about Rische, running in and declaring out of breath, "We've struck it! We've struck it!" Augusta notes she was rather frigid to him. She said to him, "Rische, when you bring me money instead of rocks, then Ill believe you."[20]

Augusta did not recognize the value of the black pebble-like sand that had put Rische in ecstasy. To her, it was the same stuff she had gone through with tweezers trying to find a speck of gold. This was the chaff, not silver. The silver existed inside the Lead Carbonate.

Augusta did not see it, but Rische and Hook knew its value.

Tabors share of the silver in the little black pellets amounted to $500,000 in the next fifteen months. With those profits he bought the Chrysolite Mine, which was another bonanza.

Tabor earned a richly deserved reputation for giving away and spending the money as fast as possible. The first benefactor was the Republican Party. Tabor's generosity within that party resulted in the party's putting him on the ticket as Lieutenant Governor in the upcoming election.

At first, he feigned indifference. He did not make one speech outside of Leadville during the entire campaign. As the election neared, he built a one-wire telegraph from Denver City. It was finished the day before the election. The telegraph sped the results to him, but because of the size of the state, it was another three or four days before all the results were in. On election day he could not resist casually sauntering by the primitive telegraph office 10 to 12 times.

Frederick Pitkin was elected Governor, and Tabor was elected Lieutenant Governor. At first, the Republicans were happy, but Augusta was suspicious. She worried that Horace did not have the training, experience, or background to be Lieutenant Governor.

Augusta's disenchantment with Horace had nothing to do with his generosity. He wanted to buy her the finest in dresses and shoes and jewelry. He also wanted to hire servants to do all the work Augusta had done since those awful days in Kansas. Augusta refused. She made him feel like his finally striking it rich and becoming famous and important beyond his wildest

Fig. 8

Horace A. W. Tabor, Lt. Governor (Colorado State Historical Society)

dreams was somehow wrong. Until then Horace had never been a success, but he had always worked. Now he was pretending to be a big shot. He spent money to impress people. He was spending money that was his, but he had not earned it. He was making a fool of himself. She loved her "Mr. T.", but she did not like Lieutenant Governor Tabor.

Tabor was perfect for the role of Silver King. Everybody was impressed. Everybody but Augusta. No matter how much he tried, he could not share his wealth with her. He spent less and less time at home and became a caricature of himself in Leadville. Some of his escapades included:

- hiring a chef from Delmonico's in New York City because he was unhappy with a meal and paying his transportation and wages to Leadville;

- providing a fire department for Leadville with "TABOR" on the backs of the men's red jerseys;

- building the biggest Opera House west of the Mississippi;

- building an enormous meeting hall he named "Wigwam," one of the few buildings that did not have TABOR in the title; and

- buying diamonds, champagne, 50-cent cigars, and any business proposition put to him.

He still could not say no.

Tabor was now on the pinnacle of his professional career. There was only one way to go and that was down. He made two decisions that made his fall particularly clumsy. Both decisions are hard to understand. Tabor finally said no. He did not say it to the crooks who were conning him out of money or to the men who just wanted gifts. He said no to the miners, the men who were actually doing the work that produced the silver, and he said no to Augusta. Since he did not have much practice at saying no, he did not understand the nuances required when using that word with his best friends, the miners in Leadville, or his family.

The lead carbonate was low grade silver. Tons were needed in order to extract the silver at the smelter. Scores of miners shoveled twelve hours a day, making $3.00 a day in wages. The work was grueling, and

Leadville was an expensive town. Everything was higher because of the added freight expense to bring the supplies to the mountain town.

The miners wanted $3.75 a day and asked that Tabor build a small hospital in Leadville. For some reason, he was suspicious of his friends and refused to give them the raise. After a little thought, he counter-offered with $2.75 a day. The miners answered his offer with a demand for $4.00 for an eight-hour day, or they would strike. His first response was to push the miners even farther away by instituting new rules. He commanded the men not to talk or smoke on their shift. If they did, they would be fired.

The Tabor Light Cavalry was already in place. Tabor started the cavalry to clean up Leadville, a pretty rough mining town. His first move was to use this private army to enforce his rules about talking and smoking. Then he enlarged the army. Tabor promoted himself to General and purchased beautiful uniforms. He and his staff wore red trousers, blue coats, and black felt hats adorned with black plumes and gold cord. The flashing steel scabbards on their belts were mounted with gold. The buckles had monograms for each individual company. One Lieutenant impressed a little girl so much that she thought she was talking to God.

The miners' strike spread to the other mines. The owners did not want to go against the magic Tabor name. His reputation at that point was that he could do no wrong in his mining decisions. Soon there were 10,000 miners on strike in the area.

Governor Pitkin was an interested spectator. His Lieutenant Governor had bitten off more than he could chew. Pitkin was told that Tabor was going to hang six of the mining union's leaders without a trial. He tried to intervene by sending troops from the Colorado militia to Leadville. They were led by David I. Cook. At first, the miners were afraid the militia would join up with Tabor's cavalry. They did not think Governor Pitkin would publicly question the Lieutenant Governor, much less go to war with the states biggest Republican campaign donor. However, Cook, after examining the facts, threw the support of the state toward the miners.

Cook did not allow any more meetings on either side and gave the miners who still wanted to work in Leadville the original $3.00 a day they were making before the strike. By this time, however, many of the miners had left the town, disgusted by the whole affair.

Augusta watched from a distance. She and her son, Maxcey, stayed in their Denver mansion. It was now time for Horace to join them in Denver. He could not show his face in Leadville. The mine owners who before had stuck with him lost all their respect for the magic Tabor name after the strike debacle.

Tabor had planned on a move to Denver anyway. He had bought a twenty room mansion from Henry Brown, builder of The Brown Palace, in 1879. Augusta was not overly impressed with the mansion. The new financial status had not dulled her wit or cost her any of her Calvinist values, "I will never go up these steps, Tabor, if you think I will ever have to go down them." She summed up the half mile separating the mansions on Capitol Hill by telling Tabor, "I would scarcely know how to return the call of the woman next door who arrived in a carriage." [21] Tabor surprised Augusta with a carriage of her own. It was an exact replica of the one driven by the White House coachmen and cost $2,000.

The second of Tabors decisions that caused his fall as the Silver King of Colorado was his marrying Baby Doe

Fig. 9
Baby Doe (Colorado Historical Society)

McCourt. Baby Doe came from the Midwest. She was married to an older man. They moved to Central City to make their fortune, but her husband continued to be a financial failure. Baby Doe knew how men looked at her when she went out or walked. She was ambitious and went to nearby Leadville to see what the fuss was about the Silver King who lived there. She expected to see an old man because of his fame and riches.

It was common knowledge that Tabor had lunch at the Clarendon. One day he made his entrance with a few of his cronies. Right next to his table was another table with a beautiful woman eating alone, Baby Doe McCourt. When Baby Doe saw Tabors regular features and magnificent mustache, she was smitten.

It did not take long before they had their lunches at the same table. Both were married to someone else. Tabor was the Lt. Governor, so they tried to be discreet. He told Baby Doe to wear thick veils when they went out to prevent their being found out. The veils could not hide her well known and much appreciated figure. Leadville loved the drama, but the attitude toward the scandal in the Denver papers was not as sophisticated and forgiving as in Leadville.

The papers loved hating it. Think of it! The Lieutenant Governor—the Silver King, a Republican—had a mistress! Tabor was not garnering future votes. His ambition at the time was to be Senator. The miners were mad because of the strike and everybody else was mad or at least embarrassed by his treatment of Augusta.

Tabor knew he had to do something majestic to buy his way out of this trouble. He decided to build the Tabor Block. "Block" was a grand term the pioneers used for business houses they built. The Tabor Block was a distinctive five-floor-high office building. It cost

$365,000. It was imposing, and the Chicago architects W. J. Edbrooke, who had designed the University of Notre Dame and buildings in Chicago, and F. P. Burnham designed the office building in Denver for Tabor.

After the office building was completed, Tabor wanted to build a grand opera house in Denver as he had in Leadville. He told Edbrooke to go to Europe for some new ideas: "Don't pattern after those chicken coups . . . but pick up any good ideas they've got laying around. Improve on them, see?"[22] Both of the architects had a nice European vacation since the plans for Tabor Opera House were drawn and locked in their desk drawer before they left.

The Opera House was almost finished when Tabor went in for an inspection. He saw a picture of Shakespeare being hung in the foyer and asked, "Who is the man in the portrait?" When told, he blew up. "Shakespeare? What did he ever do for Denver? Put my picture there."[23]

Tabor's philanthropy may have won him support in Denver if he had not brought the Baby Doe issue forward, placing it squarely on page one in Denver and every other newspaper in the country. He decided that opening night at the Opera House was the time to go public. He told Baby Doe to put her veils away. He bought her a $70,000 ermine cape and took her to opening night.

Augusta did not cry the night of the opening. She did cry when she read a report in the *News* the next morning that described the empty Tabor box. Tabor may not have been there, but there were enough flowers in the box to make it newsworthy. His timing was especially callous because Augusta had just written him a letter, pleading with him to take her to the show to stop the talk.

The next day the women gossiped about Augusta's absence at the premier. Augusta had never been a social climber, and she stayed in character. She told them she did not want their sympathies. The ladies remained firm and redoubled their efforts to shun Tabor and Baby Doe. Baby Doe had now gone public since Tabor told her to forget the veils.

From there it was only a short step to divorce. Augusta was soon disputing the validity of the divorce because she said it was not given willingly. The divorce was a long legal scandal. It took two years for the court to finalize the split in their marriage. It started in 1881 and finally ended in 1883.

In the interim, Tabor married Baby Doe in 1882 in a civil ceremony. He tried to keep the marriage secret, but his fame did not allow for secrecy. After the marriage in 1882 to Baby Doe, he was a bigamist. His political future was totally destroyed. The new scandal embarrassed the Republicans again.

Senator Teller, the widely respected representative from Central City, was appointed Secretary of the Interior by President Chester Arthur. Arthur's predecessor, John Garfield, had been assassinated after a few months in office. The Republican Party in Colorado now had the opportunity to put whomever they wanted in his now vacant Senate seat.

The Republicans wanted Tabor and Baby Doe out of town, but they did not want to give him the political plum. The compromise was to send him and Baby Doe to Washington for a term of thirty days, then replace him with George Chilcott for the remainder of the term.

It was during this thirty day term that Tabor and Baby Doe planned to marry again. The divorce with Augusta had become final. Who would notice the earlier civil marriage? He soon discovered the answer to that question was almost all the wives and many of the men in Washington. One invitation to the wedding was returned to them ripped in half.

When he remarried Baby Doe, no secrets remained about the affair. President Arthur went to the ostentatious wedding, and soon regretted it. Tabor went up and talked to the President like he was an old friend and kept slapping him on the back. Afterwards, a guilt-by-association had rubbed off on the new President.

Senator Teller was expected to go to the wedding, and he went under protest. He wrote his friend in Denver that he felt he had to go. He also noted that Mrs. Teller refused to go. Tabor is an honest man in money matters, and I believe he is truthful, but he has made a great fool of himself with reference to that woman, and he ought now to retire and attend to his private affairs [24]

Baby Doe returned to Denver after the wedding. No one visited their mansion. The excuse given to any reporter who asked why she and Tabor were not going to any parties was that she had so many invitations she did not want to go to one party and hurt the feelings of the others. This feeble attempt to hide the fact that the Senator and she were still being shunned in Denver was pulled out and used and reused.

The Republican Party did not nominate Tabor for any more races. He spent $200,000 one year trying to be elected to the senate and lost. He spent and spent and spent. He returned to his old familiar habit of saying yes to anybody who talked to him about any proposals. His lack of business acumen was a boon for the young state. He invested in gas and insurance companies, streetcar lines, ranches, irrigation ditches, toll roads, and mahogany forests in Honduras. He spent one million dollars on the Tabor Opera House, $40,000 for his mansion in Denver, and $365,000 for the Tabor Block. On one occasion, he purchased 100 peacocks for Baby Doe. He also had enormous gambling losses.

These expenditures and the dwindling profits from his mines started to put Tabor in debt. When the price of silver started to fall, some of the mines closed. His investments, which were not good in the best of times, did not show any improvement when the economic climate cooled

By the time he paid off his debts, Tabor had liquidated everything he owned. His character, or pride, or both, prevented him from going to friends and asking for help. He was broke and tried to recoup what was left of his life by working a played-out gold claim near Boulder. He never had been a good prospector, and he did not have any luck on this claim either.

Baby Doe surprised everyone during the lean years. She was young and attractive and could have improved her lot in life by dumping Tabor, but she stayed with him. They had two daughters and seemed as happy as any married couple in the settlement.

Senator William Teller, not a political supporter of Tabor's in his heyday as the Silver King, got Horace a job at the post office. He could now afford to move his family to a four room apartment in the Windsor Hotel. After selling the mansion to the creditors, he was allowed to rent a shack on the grounds for $30.00 per month, not exactly like the old days but better than scratching dirt near Boulder. He took the postmaster job seriously, even taking his lunch to work.

Tabor's dying words to Baby Doe in 1899 were, "Whatever happens, hold on to the Matchless [mine]."[25] She kept the mine, worth only sentimental value, and lived in poverty in a shack next to it in Leadville. Baby Doe died of exposure in 1934.

Augusta, meanwhile, moved to California, and her assets grew to one and a half million dollars. Her son Maxcey came back to Colorado and managed the Brown Palace Hotel. Augusta thought Baby Doe would leave Horace Tabor when the money ran out, but she was wrong.

Baby Doe married Tabor because she loved him. Even though they and their two girls lived in abject poverty, Tabor and Baby Doe never looked beyond each other for affection. The two are buried next to each other at Calumet Cemetery in Denver.Augusta is buried alone in a private cemetery.

Chapter Five

The Methodist Mafia

Colorado politics, like that of most frontier states, has always been fundamentally democratic.

—Colorado State Constitution

THE METHODIST MAFIA

William Gilpin had expected a Confederate move to Colorado Territory, and he was right. Major Henry H. Sibley commanded a large Rebel unit that was moving toward Denver. Gilpin's Lambs moved south to intercept the rebs at Glorietta Pass in New Mexico. Half of the Lambs, without concern for their own safety, attacked the larger Confederate unit. The Lambs who attacked Sibley did not have a chance. Many were killed, and Sibley thought he had won the battle. He could not hear the noise to the rear because of the sounds of the battle.

The former Methodist minister turned officer, Major John M. Chivington, had circled around behind the Southern troops and systematically destroyed everything the Rebs needed for the long march to Denver. Chivington and his Lambs shot all the Rebels' horses and donkeys. Then, they burned all the saddles, maps, and food rations the Rebel army needed for its march to Denver.

After winning the battle, Major Sibley realized he had lost the war. Major Chivington, the rotund commander in charge of killing the horses and burning the supplies, was hailed as the "Hero of Glorietta Pass."

The west portico of the Colorado capitol building in Denver honors the First Cavalry and this remarkable act of heroism. The man who designed the monument, Jack Howland, was a member of Colorado's First Cavalry.

John Evans, who had been appointed Territorial Governor by Lincoln to replace Gilpin, was nothing like Gilpin. Evans made no pretense of loving the West. He wanted the job as Territorial

Fig. 10

The Denver Bunch. Gov. John Evans, Senator Jerome Chaffee, and Col. John Chivington (The Denver Public Library, Western History Department)

Governor simply to use as a stepping stone toward becoming Senator when Colorado became a State.

Evans was forty-eight years old. He had a very long white beard and was one of the wealthiest Methodists in the Middle West. He had started a railroad as well as Northwestern University in Illinois. Evans spoke in a slow methodical way. He was born a Quaker but became a Methodist because he admired the orderly lives of the Methodists he knew in Illinois.

He was an executive, not an outdoorsman. One rumor was that he had been bitten by a mosquito on a fishing trip and since then had not ventured outside. Governor Evans did spend most of his time in his office. He befriended the popular Col. Chivington. The fellow Methodist advised Evans on the Indian problem. He told the Governor that it was the responsibility of Evans to eliminate the Indians and warned Evans that "nits make lice."[1]

Evans, an Illinois man, found it hard to understand why each Indian did not want his own white-picket-fenced farm. It was equally hard for the Indian to understand the concept of owning land. Land was for anyone to rove over in pursuit of food, buffalo, horses, friends, and enemies. When the berries had been picked, they moved on. They believed that the Indian could own a horse, but the land belonged to God.

It was inevitable that these two views about land would eventually clash. Until shortly after the Civil War, Indians were usually not a threat. They tolerated the white man's moving onto the land and declaring they owned it. Then, the white man killed off the one thing the Indian had to have to live, the buffalo. Finally, the white men who had forced the proud Indian into either begging or dying of starvation called the Indians names. The Indians, through some perverse reasoning, became known as savages by the white men.

Some Indians did force the issue. One incident took place 25 miles south of Denver on a farm. A white family of four was killed and scalped. The farming family was dumped in their well. A neighbor, disgusted by the loss of his friends, loaded the remains onto a cart and brought the mutilated bodies to

Denver. He parked his grotesque load on Larimer Street under the Governor's office.

Governor Evans could start a university or build a railroad, but there was nothing in his previous life in Illinois to prepare him for the smelly contents of the cart under his window. He and Denver reacted as if all of Denver were under attack.

The women and children were gathered and put in a central building. Then Governor Evans warned:

> Patriotic citizens of Colorado--I again appeal to you to organize for defense of your homes and families against the merciless savages . . . Any man who kills a hostile Indian is a patriot; but there are some Indians who are friendly and to kill one of these will involve us in greater difficulty. It is important therefore to fight only the hostile, and no one has been or will be restrained from this.[2]

He did not say how to tell "hostile" from "friendly" Indians. The stage was set.

The Indians Evans had seen or heard about in Illinois did not scalp farm families and dump them in the family well. He did not know what to do. He turned to Chivington for advice. The Hero of Glorietta who had already told Evans it was his responsibility to exterminate the Indians did not counsel peace. Col. Chivington told the Governor that it was time for more violence. He said if the Governor struck now, the Indians would run in terror, and the Indian menace would disappear.

Evans was invited to a meeting with seven local Indian chiefs. The Indians did not want to be shot at as "unfriendlies" any more than the pioneers wanted to be scalped. The peace talks might have resulted in a cooling down, but Evans chose to take Col. Chivington to the peace conference. The results of the talks were discouraging.

Black Feather advised the Indians to sleep together in large groups in the interest of safety. Two hundred gathered quietly at Sand Creek. Just to be on the safe side, Black Feather put a white flag on top of a Union flag. He flew them day and night over his teepee.

Black Feather was friendly to the pioneers. He had helped them in their earlier years in Denver. Once he had a tribal dance performed on one of the main streets of Denver, which was written about in the *Rocky Mountain News*.

Col. Chivington attacked the sleeping Indians with the Third Cavalry. Black Feather ran for his life after hearing gunfire. He was the only one who made it out of Sand Creek alive. Two-thirds of those massacred were mothers, children, and babies. For some reason, Chivington ordered that none of the corpses be buried. He just rode away.

The details of the massacre came out in painful detail at two congressional hearings in Washington, D.C.:

Question: Were any acts of barbarity perpetrated?

Answer: Yes, sir; I saw the bodies of those lying there all cut to pieces, worse mutilated than any I ever saw before; the women cut all to pieces.[3]

In the East, the result of the hearings was an immediate condemnation of Chivington and sympathy for the Indians. The Indians retaliated up and down the front range. Stage coach stations, farms, and travelers were all vulnerable. The Indians attacked again and again.

Flour soared to $27.00 per 100 pounds, and bacon and sugar rose to 50 cents a pound. This time the pioneers had good reason to panic. Chivington's attack on the friendlies at Sand Creek provoked the Indians. Instead of their cowering as Chivington had assured Evans, the Indians fought the whites and did an effective job of blocking a major source of Denver's food, the wagon train. They ambushed wagon trains and burned down farms. Sam Elbert, a prominent Denver Methodist, panicked. He wired Washington:

We must have five thousand troops to clean out these savages, or the people of this territory will be compelled to leave it. Everything is already at starvation prices. The General Government must help us or give up the Territory to the Indians.[4]

Despite the news of the massacre, Denver was not as quick to condemn. At first the pioneers gave Chivington the benefit of the doubt. They remembered the cart parked under the Governors window. Most still felt that Chivington had done a nasty job for them. Chivington lost this hard core western support when Captain Soule was murdered in downtown Denver.

Most people thought Chivington either shot Soule or had him shot because he was one of the Third Cavalry ordered to testify about the Sand Creek Massacre. Chivington was forced into exile. Governor Evans, who had sought advice from Chivington on Indian matters, was condemned as much as Chivington. Evans political career never recovered from the "battle" at Sand Creek.

When President Johnson decided to replace Evans, he appointed Sam Elbert to be acting Governor until he decided on a replacement. Elbert was family to Evans since he had married one of Evans' daughters. He was more than a son-in-law to John Evans. Evans truly liked Elbert.

The Civil War had just come to an end, which allowed the Army to react to the problem in the Colorado Territory. The Cavalry rode in and saved the day but not in an heroic battle. The Army built a string of forts along the original routes used by the trappers. In a quiet way the Cavalry, or "Yellow Legs" because of the stripes on their uniforms, regained control.

Evans had only wanted to be a Senator and did not mind the ignoble end to an otherwise excellent term as Territorial Governor. When Evans ran for congress, his opponents would not let him escape from the tarnish Sand Creek had created. His political ambitions were changed to that of the insider who does not run publicly. Evans built Colorado's first university, a Methodist Seminary (now Denver University), and remained politically active in Denver even though his days in elective office were over.

The leader who replaced Evans was a dapper politician who bought his clothes and got his beard trimmed in New York City. His name was Jerome Chaffee. Chaffee was one of the first men to make a fortune in Leadville. After Tabor bought out one of his partners in The Little Pittsburgh silver mine, he paid Jerome Chaffee $125,000 for part of his mine down the hill from the Little Pittsburgh. Chaffee then bought out Tabor's partner and became partners with Tabor. A third partner in The Little Pittsburgh mine was David Moffatt. He, too, made a fortune from the silver mine and spent it on building a trans-continental railroad through the mountains.

Chaffee liked politics. He was a Territorial Representative to Congress from Colorado before its statehood. His term was 1871 to 1875 as a Representative. When Colorado became a state, he got one of the most sought-after jobs in the new state, that of Senator.

Chaffee had started at the bottom in the Republican Party and methodically worked his way up to Senator. His Denver Bunch was opposed in the local legislature by the Golden [city] Bunch. William Teller, the King of Gilpin County, was the leader of this opposition.

Jerome Chaffee had supported fellow Republican John Evans when Evans was Territorial Governor. When Evans was forced into retirement by the voters, he supported Jerome Chaffee. Chaffee was from Colorado City, but they were both the "Denver Bunch" in the political sense.

Both men shared an ambition to be Senator, but Territories did not have Senators until they became states, so both Evans and Chaffee were a part of an effort to move Colorado from a Territory to a state. At first, despite their lobbying in Congress for an Enabling Act that would entitle the Territory to vote, Congress was lethargic. The Civil War occupied most of their time, and there was no reason for Colorado to become a state since it looked like Lincoln's re-election was an impossible dream.

Aside from the lack of any immediate advantage an extra state in the Republican column would offer, the Congressmen wondered why they should rush through an Enabling Act for the Territory of Colorado. The average number of years between an areas becoming a Territory and the Territory's becoming a state was thirty years. Colorado Territory had only been formed in 1861 and discovered in the political sense a few years before that.

The Union's sudden ability on the battlefield changed Lincoln's chances from impossible to inevitable, but the Republicans would need every vote in the 1864 Presidential contest they could acquire. The Republican Congress suddenly announced that Nebraska, Colorado, and Nevada were prepared to join the Union. They passed the Enabling Act of 1864 with the enthusiastic approval of President Lincoln.

At this point Chaffee and Evans congratulated each other, thinking statehood would pass in the required vote in the Territory. Their part of the Territory was enthusiastic, and Denver supported the initiative. The rest of the Territory was less sure, and the measure failed by a four to one margin. The fear of new taxes and Evans and Chaffee's tactical error of not promoting the benefits of statehood throughout the Territory cost them the election.

Chaffee and Evans were still determined to be senators. They decided to hold the election again. William Teller, the political leader of the miners in Gilpin County, was a lawyer who objected to the second election. It was one more brick in the wall the Denver Bunch was building between itself and the rest of the Territory.

The results of the second unauthorized election was that statehood won by 125 votes. The Denver Bunch were determined but were not very good at covering their tracks. The fact that many people changed positions on a vote in which they had expressed themselves a few months earlier called for some kind of examination. On closer scrutiny the Democrats claimed the "suspicious" results had been helped by some drunken Ute Indians. The Utes, apparently, were filling in the needed ballots.

Another reason for doubt was that one county did not know about the election at all, and another only found out there was an election at noon. The totals did not reflect that two counties did not vote. The Denver Group thought no one would care how they got the votes as long as they had the majority. But they were thwarted again. This time it was national politics that dashed their hopes.

The Republican congress originally passed the Enabling Act of 1864 to get the votes that might be needed to re-elect Lincoln. After Lincoln's election and assassination, the tables were turned. The Democratic Vice President, Andrew Johnson, was being impeached by the Republicans because of his soft attitude toward the South.

Johnson did not want more Republicans in Congress because they were impeaching him. The House of Representatives impeached Johnson, and when the vote went to the Senate, Johnson only survived by one vote. If Chaffee and Evans had been in the Senate and voted with the party, which is likely, Johnson would have been impeached.

Johnson, helped by William Teller, vetoed Colorado's Enabling Act. It had now been defeated at home and in Washington, but Chaffee and Evans were not to be denied. They did not accept what was apparent to everyone else in the country. They opened offices in Washington. Evans and Chaffee wore black frock coats and were addressed by fellow Coloradoans as "Senator." They went to Congress and tried to mingle but were ignored by the Senators who had attained their offices in the more traditional way.

In 1875, a Republican Congress, the President, and Colorado Territory approved statehood for Colorado. Chaffee finally became Senator.

The first two territorial governors in Colorado had been capable, intelligent men. Gilpin was more the western idealist than Evans, and Evans was a better executive than Gilpin, but both were well received by the pioneers. The third territorial governor was appointed by President Johnson in 1865. Alexander Cummings was a tax collector from Pennsylvania. Cummings was known as a politician with a questionable reputation. The *Mining Register* in Central City rejoiced when he returned to Pennsylvania for another political job in the East. The delighted editor of the *Mining Register* told his readers: "Glorious News! Good-bye to Cummings! He is sent to curse Pennsylvania. Let the Lord be Praised!"

Cummings was followed in 1867 by A. Cameron Hunt. Hunt was governor until 1869. His successor was Edward McCook. The pioneers distrusted the elegant and sophisticated McCook. They were also suspicious of his beautiful young bride because of the decolletage on her dresses and the way she flaunted her diamonds. When a handsome Russian prince was visiting, McCook's wife fainted right into the prince's arms. The wives of the pioneers were offended and snipped at the Territory's first lady for doing something they all wished they had thought to do themselves.

McCook and his wife were not hard working or popular, so Chaffee convinced President Grant to replace McCook. Grant did not think McCook was worth fighting over and replaced him with one of Chaffee's Denver Bunch, the hard working and popular Sam Elbert who was the acting governor when Evans had to step down because of the Sand Creek Massacre.

Ten months later Chaffee, Grant, and a few others were playing poker during one of their regular Sunday poker games.

> Chaffee angered the President by filling an inside straight over Grants three-of-a-kind. The pot was large and the alleged outcome was that poor Elbert, an honest, well-meaning man, found himself out of office and McCook back in just as Sam was beginning to enjoy the governorship. [5]

President Lincoln had caved in to pressure and replaced Gilpin. President Johnson blamed the Sand Creek Massacre on Evans, and now President Grant was punishing a third good man because he lost a poker hand. Fortunately for Colorado, the territorial days were almost over. Presidents would no longer pick and choose its governors.

With statehood imminent, the politicians started writing the first State Constitution. The largest vocational group at the constitutional convention were lawyers. It was one of the longest constitutions in the country.

Colorado became a state in 1876, exactly one hundred years after the country's first birthday. The "Centennial State" did not officially join the Union until August 1, 1876, but it celebrated on the Fourth of July, 1876.

ITEMS IN THE FIRST COLORADO STATE CONSTITUTION

- Theft of any domestic animal valued at more than $10.00 was punishable by a jail sentence of 20 years or by death.

- Altering a brand (rustling) brought 1-5 years in prison.

- For counterfeiting coins or gold dust the penalty was one to fourteen years.

- For mixing base metals (usually brass filings) with gold dust, $1,000 fine or five years in jail.

- Use of false scales to weigh gold dust brought a fine of $500.00 or six months in jail.

Chapter Six

The Golden Bunch

The past may have been bad; the present may still be worse; but there is the ILEGANT FUTURE

—Anonymous Miner

THE GOLDEN BUNCH

The pioneers had shown from the outset a distinct liking for party life. Accounts abound about all-night dances. So, when Statehood was finally attained in 1876, Colorado had reports of a magnificent parade and picnic on the Fourth of July, and it is likely violins and wash tub basses screeched and plucked until sun-up on the fifth.

The settlers could be proud. Things were different because of their endurance. Emigration to all parts of the state was causing the state to grow. The railroad had its ups and downs, but now there were tracks laid, and people could move to Colorado in a matter of days, not months.

The two powerful and ambitious leaders, Jerome Chaffee and Henry Teller had vied with each other in the past decade for political support. This sometimes bitter struggle within the Republican Party, along with the opposition of the voters in the southern part of the Territory, had scuttled the statehood aspirations of the Denver Bunch in an election September 13, 1864.

After the second suspicious election, which had not been called for in the Enabling Act, Teller changed from a pro-statehood stance on the original bill to not being for statehood in the second election. The change was probably brought on by a mix of things. One, the Denver Bunch had grossly overestimated the population. Two, the second election was clearly illegal before any votes were counted, and many of those votes that were counted were suspicious. Three, the second time around after the original defeat, Chaffee and Evans recommended they be the new state's first senators. Teller wanted to be a senator as much as Chaffee, and when Chaffee realized his mistake in not putting Teller in the revised

Fig. 11

The Golden Bunch. Senator Henry Moore Teller; W.A. H. Loveland, Founder of Golden; and Edward Berthoud, railroad pioneer. (The Denver Public Library, Western History Department.)

act as Senator, he offered Teller a seat in the lower house. Teller turned him down flat.

Teller was a lawyer. He took pride in his abilities and showed that pride when he was graduating from law school in New York. Bar exams were optional at the time, and he insisted on the trip to Binghamton, New York to take the exams. He did well on them.

In Colorado, Teller is remembered for the law of Apex. In it a miner could follow a vein of gold off of his claim to wherever the vein led.

Teller did not approve of the second statehood election but had just ten months earlier crossed the state, promoting statehood. He was not sure how to show his new attitude toward statehood, so he just said nothing. The miners understood, took his silent lead, and voted against statehood.

When the Denver Bunch "won" this second election, Teller went to Washington. Lincoln had just been assassinated and a very unpopular Democrat, Johnson, was trying to make peace with the South. Johnson did not want the South to be treated as traitors to the country nor did he want to send more troops into the South. As a result, he was vilified in the press and cartoons and was impeached in the House of Representatives.

The impeachment trial was going on in the Senate when Teller arrived from Colorado Territory. Seats in the gallery were impossible to get, and talking to one of the Senators was impossible. He finally got the ear of Senator Conkling, a senator from his old home state, New York. Senator Conkling agreed to put Tellers argument in the Congressional Record since it was impossible for a Senator to talk about anything but impeachment at that time in the Senate.

President Johnson was following the impeachment proceedings. He knew his detractors had momentum and an enormous number of votes; consequently, he did not look forward to Colorado's entering the fray with two more Republican votes. Johnson announced he was forced to veto the bill for statehood because of the second election and because he thought Colorado's population had been exaggerated. The population needed a recount in the next census. The figure in the census demanded by Johnson was much closer to Tellers estimate of 35,000 to 40,000 than Chaffee's 75,000 to 100,000. Yet, that should not have mattered because there was nothing in the Constitution requiring a certain number of bodies before a Territory could apply for statehood.

Evans cried foul, which was a little bit like the pot calling the kettle black after his suspicious election. There was nothing Chaffee could do. The Golden Bunch, led by Teller, had adroitly outmaneuvered him. Teller had given Johnson what he needed in order to veto. Colorado remained a Territory.

Evans was not the only one to condemn Teller for his trip to Washington. The *Rocky Mountain News* attacked Teller more viciously than at any other time before or after:

> In former days he did have some respect, where now is man so mean as to do him honor? The brand of Cain is upon him... Let the curse of every citizen be upon him. Let him be a dead man among us, so vile, so corrupt, so offensive, that the very mention of his name will excite loathing. Let the guilt of his own base acts be made to weigh so heavily upon him that he will be only too glad to escape where he cannot even hear the name of the Territory he has so abused.[2]

The state used Teller as a scapegoat, but his core of support in the mining district supported him even though they did not fully understand what his motives were.

Henry Teller was born the oldest boy in a poor, Dutch farming family in New York. He had no natural inclination to move to the West as many of his neighbors were doing. His law partner, Hiram Johnson, nagged him to come out as a tourist, and if he did not like the area, Johnson would stop pestering him to come. Teller resisted but finally agreed to a one month trial. He was not overly impressed as he rode the long trip westward. Pausing in Denver City for only a short respite, he finished the trip by way of Golden City and finally reached the Gregory "Diggings."

Hiram Johnson had been right. Teller fell in love with life in a gold camp. He wrote to his fiance that he wanted to live with her in the Rocky Mountains. He then went back home and married her. The two were not feeling well when they got married. Mrs. Teller remembered:

> The wedding took place in our home, but it was not a very joyous occasion. Mr. Teller had suffered a serious illness soon after coming to Colorado and his recovery has been slow. At the time of the wedding he was almost without color and as thin as a rail. My sister had just died of Galloping Consumption (tuberculosis) and my own health was so precarious that I was believed to be coming down with that fatal disease. I was as pale as the bridegroom, and people generally remarked that never had they seen such a hopeless looking couple so far as appearance is concerned. To our friends the proposed journey more than half way across the country, much of it by stage over barren and uninhabited plains, seemed a desperate undertaking. Many were the predictions that neither of us would ever again see New York State.[3]

Teller was sometimes addressed as General since he had been appointed a General during the Sand Creek Massacre. Most of Central City simply called him H. M. Mrs. Teller was a Methodist. H. M. went to church with her but never formally joined that or any other church. He did not seem to enjoy the trips to the mountains, but once established in Central City, Teller enjoyed traveling, and liked nothing better than to sit beside the driver of the stagecoach during the daylight hours of the trip. [4]

Another man who enjoyed riding on the top of the stagecoach was from London. General Charles Palmer was resting on the top of the stage on a beautiful starlit night near what is now Colorado Springs. He told himself that it was so beautiful he would return to the area. He later built a narrow gauge railroad into the area and the adjacent mountains. The name Colorado City did not sound right to him. He thought if he changed the name to Colorado Springs, his friends in London

Fig. 12
William J. Palmer (Colorado Historical Society)

might visit. Therefore, he changed the name to Colorado Springs despite the fact that there were no springs in the city.

So many people visited from London and liked Colorado Springs, that its nickname became Little London. One hazard on General Palmer's narrow gauge train was the wind. The tracks were so narrow and the train so light that more than once a wind blew the entire train off its narrow gauge tracks.

When Palmer retired, he became president at the School of Mines. He took his job as president seriously, too seriously his students thought. They complained about the homework requirements. When he did not back down they threatened to quit:

> Mines completed the old century with 244 students, not all of whom were amenable to the no-nonsense standards imposed by the current President, Charles S. Palmer. In February, 1900, the entire freshman class walked out in protest over the rigor of their assignments, but neither administration nor trustees gave in, and those students who did ultimately choose to return were obligated to re-register.[5]

One of the key members of the western bunch of politicians, Edward Berthoud, was on the board of trustees of the school at the time. Berthoud supported Palmer. Berthoud was a quiet sort of team player. He also supported A. H. Loveland, the founder of Golden, in the intrigues between Golden and Denver. Berthoud tried to stay in the background but was a key member of the Golden Bunch because of his experience as an engineer and surveyor for railroads. Like Gilpin, he had some ideas that were grandiose. Gilpin wanted to build railroads to Europe and then build a bridge to England. Berthoud wanted to cross the steep Rockies with a system of inclined planes and machines to tow the trains up and over the peaks. Neither idea was employed.

Berthoud did work on one of the first narrow gauge common carriers in the world with tracks one foot eleven inches apart. The concept of a narrow gauge was exactly what was needed in the Rockies. The track was lighter and did not require as much room as the standard gauge, and the rolling stock was lighter.

Loveland sold the miners goods as they went into the mountains, then with Berthoud's help built a narrow gauge railroad to the mining camps. He talked Union Pacific's Jay Gould into a lucrative deal for Golden. Loveland graded the land between Golden and Cheyenne, and the Union Pacific put down the tracks and supplied the rolling stock. When Gould eventually wanted some control over his investment, Loveland and Berthoud tried to deny him access to the line. Gould was not to be denied, and he eventually took his railroad back from Loveland and Berthoud.

The link with Cheyenne Depot soon gave access to both coasts. The Central Pacific, with its Chinese laborers, met the Union Pacific with their track, laid primarily by the Irish, at Promontory Point, Utah, on May 10, 1869.

The steam engines faced each other with steam hissing out of their engines. Before the telegraphers could announce to the waiting world that the road had been completed, the golden stake had to be driven home. The President of the Central Pacific took the sledge hammer with the appropriate solemnity. He raised it back, brought it forward, and missed the stake. He handed the sledge hammer to his counterpart from the Union Pacific. Vice President Thomas Durant tried—and missed. To the roar of laughter, Durant passed the sledge hammer to his chief engineer. Grenville Dodge slammed the stake home, and now the telegraphers could send out to the world: "The Pacific railroad is done."[6]

Before the joining of the tracks, the trip across the country had taken three months. Now it only took eight days. Gilpin's forecasts seemed to be coming true.

Chapter Seven

PANIC!

All men of virtue and intelligence know that all the ill of life—scarcity of money, baldness, the common bacillus, Home Rule, and the potato bug—are due to the Sherman bill. If it is repealed, sin and death will vanish from this world. . . . the skies will fall, and we shall all catch larks.[1]

PANIC!

John Hay could enjoy a good laugh when writing about the repeal of the Sherman Bill. He was an Easterner, and the price of silver did not seem like something that would affect him.

When the Eastern Republican John Sherman offered his bill to the Senate for consideration, William Teller only gave it his lukewarm support. He felt it was a "sop" being offered to the West in order to prevent any hard feelings about Congress demonetizing silver. Teller was an "off ox" on the Sherman Bill because he wanted to fix the problem. He was for bimetallism and wanted the country to return to the time honored system of using two metals. In that way if there were a problem in supplying one ore, the other would fill the gap until the first one was again mined successfully.

The United States used the two metal system until 1873. Congress, in an act that Westerners later decried as the "Crime of 1873," removed the requirement that a stipulated amount of silver be in each coin pressed in this country. Little attention was paid to the bill at the time because Colorado was enjoying a silver boom. The miners did not need the government to buy their silver because they were selling it to industry for higher prices than the government support.

The mines in Colorado in the 1870s were so attractive that the Republican governor, John L. Routt, left the smoky air of the statehouse for the clear air of the mountains and mined for silver. He was not alone. Thousands of miners poured into Poverty Gulch to try their luck. Millions of dollars worth of silver were extracted and processed in the 1870s.

The government paid the silver miner $1.29 an ounce until 1873. The law of supply and demand with so many people mining incredible amounts of silver started to force the price of silver down. Then, when the price was nearing $1.29 an ounce, the silver miners realized what Congress had done in 1873. The miners could not even get the $1.29 per ounce from the government. hey saw it as a plot by Eastern congressmen and London financiers.

The miners complained loudly and bitterly about the law they called "The Crime of 1873." They said the law demonetizing silver was unconstitutional. They wrote letters, lobbied, pleaded, and got nowhere. The politicians who had created the problem with the Coinage Act in 1873 showed little remorse.

IN CHICAGO MARKETS			
Year			
1872.... 19.3 .70	1.47	1.32	
1873.... 18.8 .62	1.31	1.29	
1874.... 15.4 .72	1.43	1.27	
1875.... 15.0 .85	1.12	1.24	
1876.... 12.9 .67	1.24	1.15	
1877.... 11.8 .54	1.17	1.20	
1878.... 11.1 .56	1.34	1.15	
1879.... 9.9 .47	1.07	1.12	
1880.... 11.5 .54	1.25	1.14	
1881.... 11.4 .55	1.11	1.13	
1882.... 11.4 .67	1.19	1.13	
1883.... 10.8 .68	1.13	1.11	
1884.... 10.5 .61	1.07	1.01	
1885.... 10.6 .54	.86	1.06	
1886.... 9.9 .50	.87	.99	
1887.... 9.5 .48	.89	.97	
1888.... 9.8 .56	.85	.93	
1889.... 9.9 .47	.90	.93	
1890.... 10.2 .49	.83	1.04	
1891.... 6.0 .41	.85	.90	

The Rocky Mountain News, Dec.4,

The compromise solutions which did not address the root of the problem, a need to return to bimetallism, were the Bland Allison Act in 1873 and the Sherman Bill in 1890. They were price supports for silver but maintained gold as the only coin of the realm.

According to the *News*, the dropping silver price was directly correlated to farm prices. On December 4, 1892, it published the accompanying table on page one with the following explanation:

The above table illustrates the relation between the current price of silver and the market price of staple products of the farm. The figures given are the average quotations for each year. They plainly show the cause of the agricultural depression, and explain the burden of rural indebtedness, with interest exactions and mortgage foreclosures that are fast changing

American farm property into tenant holdings ... and reduced the inmates (of the farms) to wretchedness and want.[2]

The Eastern bankers and the Democratic President Grover Cleveland combined in an effort to discredit silver. The bankers, or "Wall Street" as Teller called them, wanted gold to be the only currency so that its value would increase without silver's competition.

The Southern and Western voters did not agree. They liked the chance to mine silver and felt the U. S. should emulate Mexico and use silver as the single ore used in currency.

The split between rich and poor, farm and city, North and South was reminiscent of the country before the Civil War. It was all the congressmen could talk about. William Jennings Bryan, a religious patriot from the Midwest, inspired two hours of cheering in the Democratic Convention in 1896 when he pleaded with the bankers: "You shall not press down upon the brow of labor this crown of thorns ... You shall not crucify mankind on a cross of gold."[3]

When the tumult slowed and the bands stopped playing, Bryan was told they would nominate him for President then and there by acclamation, but Bryan said, "If the people want me nominated, and that feeling could not endure overnight, it would perish before the campaign was a week old."[4]

During the earlier years of this battle, Teller became active in the fight for bimetallism. The last political skirmish he had been in had been the one with Chaffee over the question of statehood. Most of the time in between had been spent either as Senator or the Secretary of the Interior. President Arthur was James Garfield's Vice President. The conservative wing of the Republican party promoted his candidacy for the second spot on the ticket even though Arthur was promoting a third term for President Grant.

Garfield was shot by an anarchist, and Arthur became President. Teller knew of the gossip about the unpopular president, but he respected Arthur more than any other politician. Teller tried to help Arthur by securing his candidacy in the Republican National Convention in 1884. Teller also wanted to have a voice in who would replace his arch Senate rival, Nathaniel P. Hill. Teller tried to stack the state's department appointments in Colorado in his favor. He wrote his friend Dawson: "If I do appoint any man who is not my personal or political friend in Colorado, it will be because I am not informed of his status."[5] Despite the efforts of Teller and his friends, Arthur did not carry Colorado.

Teller's last Republican term in the Senate took him from the Secretary of the Interior to the upper House. He was taking the seat his opponent Hill had used. Teller got together with Chaffee and said he would have preferred to retire, but he was the only Republican the other candidates could endorse. Chaffee was unable to run another campaign for the Senate for himself because of his health.

The debate over the use of silver in currency did not start on the presidential level until after Grover Cleveland had been elected in 1892. The Democrat, Cleveland, and the Republican, James Blaine, spent the entire campaign debating the tariff. Four years earlier, the Republicans had drastically raised the tariff.

The Democratic platform in that election year said it preferred both gold and silver to be used as standard money. Both candidates in the major parties were out of touch with an important issue developing in the country. The third-party candidate, James Weaver, campaigned for free silver under the Populist banner. He was the first third-party candidate to receive any electoral votes since the Civil War.

Teller did not consider himself an authority on the silver question until 1888. At that time most of the West was still divided into Territories. Since they were not represented in the Senate, Teller often spoke for other Western territories as well as Colorado.

When Teller was appointed to the cabinet by President Chester Arthur, he spent long days, often averaging fourteen to sixteen hours, resolving legal questions. He spent a lot of time on homesteading questions and the problems relating to Indian schools and Reservations. He represented miners when he practiced law in Central City but did not study the monetary aspects of silver and gold.

When the first Price Support Bill was discussed in congress in 1878, Teller approached the monetary questions in a scholarly manner. Being a businessman and a conservative, he did not discount what the bankers said in their arguments. He studied both sides, and after learning as much as he could from what was available, he subscribed to and read the leading American financial papers, the English *Economist and Statist,* and the French *LEconomiste.* After this study, Teller was convinced that what was best for Colorado was also best for the United States and the world. He even sounded a little defensive in the senate when he stated:

> I admit that if I had not lived in a silver-producing State I might never have had my attention directed to this subject. I might have been willing ... to accept the statements of doctrinaires and ill-informed people as facts; but if my attention had been directed to it and I have studied it as I have studied it, I would have the same views if I lived in Connecticut that I have living in Colorado.[6]

Teller's uncompromising conviction that bimetallism was vital to economic growth was matched by President Cleveland's uncompromising stance against silver. After Cleveland was elected in 1892, bankers advised him that the current economic problems were the fault of the Sherman Silver Purchase Act. The Sherman Act did not legislate a return to bimetallism, but it did support the price of silver by mandating that the government buy some each month.

Cleveland did not have the votes to repeal the Sherman Act. He started a public relations program against silver that worried the country. A cloud of apprehension seemed to settle over the country, not that a revision of the tariff or a new monetary system was in itself feared, but blind uncertainty as to the future paralyzed action.[7]

The banking houses exerted pressure on silver by not recognizing the perfectly legal Silver Certificates. At the same time, in India, a silver mint was closed down. The price of silver continued to drop. Some of the larger mines started to close as the price of silver fell. The downward spiral on the price of silver forced more mines out of business, and the businesses that were closely related to the mines started to suffer.

In October, 1893, the tiny state of Colorado in relation to population was third in the country in closed bank liabilities, and the general business closure was over twice that of the rest of the country. The Populist Governor, Davis H. Waite, addressed a state-wide mass meeting in Denver. It was quoted throughout the country as a Call to Arms :

> Our weapons are arguments and the ballot a free ballot and a fair count. And if the money power shall attempt to sustain its usurpations by the strong hand, we shall meet that issue when it is forced upon us, for it is better, infinitely better, that blood should flow to the horses' bridles than your national liberties should be destroyed.[8]

The next day the convention had cooled down and only asked for calm consideration before destroying silver as money. Teller did not attend that convention or another one supporting free silver that was held in Chicago. He returned to Washington to prepare for the difficult legislative fight. Until now Teller had been able to look at the questions about currency as a statesman. His goals had been for the common good. With unemployment in Colorado between 30,000 and 50,000 in a state with no more than half a million total population, Teller now was motivated by concern for his fellow Coloradoans. He, personally, did not like the bill he would have to defend. He wanted a return to bimetallism. The Sherman Act did not accomplish that goal, but it did force the government to buy silver, and it did help hold the price of silver up because of this artificial support.

President Cleveland accepted what the bankers told him, not thinking that perhaps their motives might have been selfish.

When a reporter asked Teller about contradicting the President, he told the reporter that because President Cleveland's premises were wrong, his conclusions about silver naturally were wrong.

In Congress, both houses debating the silver issue were at their best. The most persuasive, though, was William Jennings Bryan. His reasoning and strong oratorical statements in objecting to the repeal of the Sherman Purchase Act resulted in the administrations singling Bryan out for punishment.

In Nebraska, the Democratic postmasters' jobs were being postponed, and applicants were forced to work against Bryan for repeal even before the appointments were handed down. The votes in Congress that Teller had counted on to make repeal impossible started to dribble away. Some Congressmen were concerned that the patronage system, which rewarded their friends and family with jobs, would be used against them to withhold jobs. Others worried about their own jobs. The press was one-sided and attacked Teller and his fellow congressmen who wanted to protect the silver miner as un-American. The articles also called them fanatics and lunatics.

The stress of the almost daily attacks from the press and the President as well as the dwindling support of congressmen on whom Teller had counted wore Teller down:

> As he proceeded he became more and more wrought up to a pitch of intensity unlike anything ever seen on the floor. He paced up and down the narrow space behind his desk earnestly gesticulating, while with a voice tremulous with emotion and his eyes wet with tears, he pictured the misery he saw in the future for the people whom he loved. The spectacle was so striking and unusual that it riveted the attention of every Senator.

The words poured forth from Mr. Tellers lips in a passionate torrent, so carried away was he with his theme, and when with clenched fist he denounced the damnable bill, the galleries burst forth with applause... When he concluded he sank to his seat buried his face in his hands, and presented a living picture of the misery he had so touchingly described.[9]

The situation for the silver men deteriorated to the point that their only hope to keep the Sherman Act from being repealed was not to let their opponents have the floor of the Senate. The purpose was not to out-wait the opposition but to keep the repeal effort in Congress until it was modified. They achieved this goal when a compromise was suggested, but the compromise was rejected by Cleveland.

After weeks of abuse in the press, Isham G. Harris told the leader of the silver Republicans, "I told you we would stay with you till hell froze over. We have had another look at our hand and must lay down."[10]

The Populists in the silver group wanted to continue the filibuster, but Teller objected. Without the support of the Democrats, nothing positive could be accomplished by continuing with the filibuster. The Free Silver Amendment lost 28 to 39. After the defeat, some silver men spoke eloquently, and others threatened what would happen to the Republic with this new law.

On October 27, 1893, Teller rose in a silent chamber and stated:

> We are neither cast down nor dejected.... We do not disguise the fact that we are to go through the valley and the shadow of death. We know what it means to turn out 200,000 silver miners in the fall of the year ... we are ready and willing to meet the occasion ... But, Mr. President, the iron will enter into our souls. We shall not forget that in this contest ... the men with whom we have stood shoulder to shoulder in the economic battles heretofore, have almost to a man forsaken us.[11]

Teller acknowledged the full defeat on the repeal of the Sherman Act. He objected to continuing the filibuster.

The people in Denver did not see Teller as a loser. His withstanding the assaults of the Eastern press in a lost cause earned the respect of every Coloradoan. On his return to Denver, he told the adoring crowd Colorado would "suffer somewhat by the repeal of the Silver Purchase Act, yet Colorado ... is not destroyed, nor even in any way permanently injured ... If we cannot mine silver at a profit ... we can mine iron, coal, and gold, and we will have prosperity and riches."12

In the next Republican nominating convention, Teller walked out with 23 other pro silver Republicans. After he founded the National Silver Party, he joined with the Democrats at their convention. Most Democrats shared his view about silver.

While Teller was a hero in defeat, Cleveland, the victor in the fight over the Sherman bill could not even regain the nomination of his party. When Cleveland was not renominated, serious thought was given to nominating the tall statesman from Colorado.

Teller did not get his hopes up, however. He did not think the Democrats would pick him, an outspoken conservative Republican, to be at the top of their ticket. As it turned out William Jennings Bryan took the same issue and used it to gain the nomination. There was no doubt after Bryan's "Cross of Gold" speech. Teller was delighted to have Bryan running and predicted he would be the next president. The Republicans outspent Bryan 12 to 1 and barely won the election. Bryan had more people voting for him in a losing cause than any other candidate who had won the Presidency. He might have won, except the economy which had teetered and tottered for years under Cleveland finally started to rebound a few months before the election.

As for Colorado, her aspirations to return to the good old days when Horace (Haw) Tabor was Silver King were squashed when Bryans hard fought campaign was not enough to take the White House. For the first time, Colorados silver output dropped. The toal silver output for the decade ending in 1890 was $19,540,000. After the panic and the repeal of the Sherman Act in the nineties, the total dropped to $12,609,000 for the ten years ending in 1900, and $4,595,000 in 1910.13 Tellers predictions were correct. The production of gold increased seven-fold between 1890 and 1900, and lead almost doubled.

When the filibuster caved in on the mining hopes of Western silver miners, the headline for the *Rocky Mountain News* on page one boldly told its readers, "IT IS FINISHED." But the Westerners knew better. When they walked 600 miles across Kansas, they made the trip bearable by having parties. When they set up primitive diggings so they could work in the mines all day, they got out the fiddles and danced all night. It is no surprise that at this apocalyptic time in their history they threw a party for their hard working senior senator. Teller was treated to a gala reception in the Brown Palace Hotel. The people got out the marching band, shook his hand, gave laudatory speeches, and sprinkled flowers on him.

REFERENCES

Chapter One

[1]Marshall Sprague, Colorado: A History (New York: W. W. Norton and Company, 1984) 12.

[2]Edward Buscombe, The BFI Companion to the Western (New York: Macmillan Publishing Company, 1988) 121.

[3]Leroy R. Hafen, Colorado and Its People: A Narrative and Topical History of the Centennial State, Vol. 1 (New York: Lewis Historical Publishing Company, 1948) 93.

[4]Herman J. Viola, Exploring the West (Washington, D.C.: Smithsonian Books, 1987) 67.

[5]Zethyl Gates, Mariano Medina (Boulder, CO: Johnson Publishing Company, 1981) 10.

[6]Viola 106.

[7]Gates 11.

[8]Jay Monaghan, Book of the American West (New York: Bonanza Books, 1963) 35.

[9]Mody C. Boatright, Folk Laughter on the American Frontier (New York: Macmillan Company, 1949) 88.

[10]Boatright 93.

[11]Boatright 93.

[12]Hafen, Vol. 1, 275.

[13]Hafen, Vol. 1, 145.

[14]Hafen, Vol. 1, 22.

[15]William Byers, ed., Rocky Mountain News, 14 May 1859: 2.

[16]Hafen, Vol. 2, 248.

[17]Hafen, Vol. 2, 253.

[18]Hafen, Vol. 2, 253.

[19]Hafen, Vol. 1, 192-193.

[20]Hafen, Vol. 2, 557.

[21]Hafen, Vol. 2, 557.

[22]Hafen, Vol. 1, 193.

[23]Hafen, Vol. 1, 375.

Chapter Two

[1]Paul F. Boller, Jr., Presidential Campaigns (New York: Oxford University Press, 1984) 95.

[2]Boller 95.

[3]Boller 94.

[4]Clifton Daniel, Chronicle of America (Kisko, NY: Prentice Hall, 1989) 270.

[5]Daniel 347.

[6]Boller 92.

[7]Boller 93.

[8]Boller 98.

[9]Boller 94.

[10]Daniel 354.

[11]Daniel 354.

[12]Boller 100.

[13]Boller 100.

[14]Boller 105.

[15]Boller 110.

[16]Boller 115.

[17]Boller 116.

[18]Boller 118.

[19]Daniel 391.

Chapter Three

[1]Harry Hansen, Colorado: A Guide to the Highest State (New York: Hastings House, 1941) 43.

[2]Leroy R. Hafen, Colorado and Its People: A Narrative and Topical History of the Centennial State, Vol. 1 (New York: Lewis Historical Publishing Company, 1948) 290-291.

[3]Hafen, Vol. 1, 231.

[4]Hafen, Vol. 2, 559.

[5]Hafen, Vol. 1, 192.

[6]Carl Ubbelohde, A Colorado History (Boulder, CO: Pruett Publishing, 1976) 94.

[7]Ubbelohde 269.

[8]Hafen, Vol. 1, 199.

[9]Caroline Bancroft, "History of Denver," Historical Encyclopedia of Colorado, ed. Thomas Chamberlin (Denver, CO: Colorado Historical Association, 1975) 168.

[10]Howard Louis Conrad, Uncle Dick Wooten: The Pioneer Frontiersman of the Rocky Mountain Region (Chicago: University of Nebraska Press, 1957) 266.

[11]William Byers, ed., Rocky Mountain News 11 June 1859: 3.

[12]Mody C. Boatright, Folk Laughter on the American Frontier (New York: Macmillan Company, 1949) 97.

[13]Boatright 108-109.

[14]Boatright 107-108.

[15]Boatright 124.

[16]Boatright 119.

[17]Boatright 116-117.

Chapter Four

[1]Robert L. Brown, The Great Pikes Peak Gold Rush (Caldwell,OH: Caxton, 1985) 31.

[2]Leroy R. Hafen, Colorado and Its People: A Narrative and Topical History of the Centennial State, Vol. 1 (New York: Lewis Historical Publishing Company, 1948) 147-149.

[3]Brown 47-50.

[4]Brown 45.

[5]Hafen, Vol. 1, 172.

[6]Hafen, Vol. 1, 175.

[7]Hafen, Vol. 1, 175.

[8]William Byers, ed., Rocky Mountain News 21 September 1863: 2.

[9]Courier Times 21 June 1887: 1.

[10]William H. Axford, Gilpin County Gold (Chicago: Sage Press, 1976) 41.

[11]Axford 43.

[12]Don Griswold and Jean Griswold, Colorado's Century of "Cities" (NP, 1958), 54.

[13]Axford 43.[12]

[14]Axford 43.

[15]Elmore Ellis, Henry Moore Teller: Defender of the West (Caldwell, OH: Caxton, 1941) 31.

[16]Carl Ubbelohde, A Colorado History (Boulder, CO: Pruett Publishing, 1976) 209-210.

[17]David Karsner, Silver Dollar (New York: Crown Publishers, 1932) 12.

[18]Caroline Bancroft, Augusta Tabor: Her Side of the Scandal (Boulder, CO: Johnson Publishers, 1955) 10.

[19]Bancroft 10.

[20]Bancroft 11.

[21]Bancroft 12.

[22]Karsner 179.

[23]Karsner 184.

[24]Ellis 155.

[25]Karsner 283.

Chapter Five

[1]Marshall Sprague, Colorado: A History (New York: W. W. Norton and Company, 1984) 39.

[2]Leroy R. Hafen, Colorado and Its People: A Narrative and Topical History of the Centennial State, Vol. 1 (New York: Lewis Historical Publishing Company, 1948) 311.

[3]Hafen, Vol. 1, 316.

4Hafen, Vol. 1, 317.

[5]Sprague 72.

Chapter Six

[1]Frank Waters, Midas of the Rockies (Chicago: Swallow Press, 1937) 84.

[2]Elmore Ellis, Henry Moore Teller: Defender of the West (Caldwell, OH: Caxton, 1941) 75-76.

[3]Ellis 41.

[4]Ellis 57.

[5]Robert C. Black III, Railroad Pathfinder: The Life and Times of Edward L. Berthoud (Evergreen, CO: Cordillera Press, Inc., 1988) 118.

[6]Clifton Daniel, Chronicle of America (Kisko, NY: Prentice Hall, 1989) 410.

Chapter Seven

[1]Elmore Ellis, Henry Moore Teller: Defender of the West (Caldwell, OH: Caxton, 1941) 218.

[2]William Byers, ed., Rocky Mountain News, 4 December 1859: 1.

[3]Clifton Daniel, Chronicle of America (Kisko, NY: Prentice Hall, 1989) 511.

[4]Daniel 511.

[5]Ellis 156.

[6]Ellis 185.

[7]Ellis 213.

[8]Ellis 217.

[9]Ellis 221-222.

[10]Ellis 226.

[11]Ellis 225-226.

[12]Ellis 228.

[13]Ellis 235.